DON'T YOU BELONG TO ME?

Don't You Belong to Me?

A Monk of New Clairvaux

PAULIST PRESS
New York/Ramsey/Toronto

Library of Congress
Catalog Card Number: 79-88985

ISBN: 0-8091-2217-0

Published by Paulist Press
Editorial Office: 1865 Broadway, New York, N.Y. 10023
Business Office: 545 Island Road, Ramsey, N.J. 07446

Printed and bound in the
United States of America

Contents

Although it seems the height of presumption,
this book is lovingly dedicated to

JESUS

with public testimony of my faith and love.

"Thank you for the free gift of your gracious birth, God, Son of Man, through which we have access to that grace in which we stand and in which we are confident of attaining glory as the sons of God. It is indeed an admirable commerce to take flesh and bestow divinity. . . ."

Blessed Guerric of Igny
Cistercian Fathers Series
vol. 8, page 48

CUM APPROBATIONE ABBATIS

My Gratitude

I would like to take this occasion to voice my thanks to many of my confreres at New Clairvaux who have helped me in various ways to bring these pages to print, especially Brothers Peter, Paul, Mark, Greg, Henri, Laurin, Anthony, David, Diego, Damien, Gerald and John. Anthony pointed out unwitting confusions in the text and in general played the "devil's advocate." David corrected much of my atrocious syntax and barbaric punctuation, saving the reader no little exasperation. After a time, due to the pressures of his own work, he left me to my own devices, and so the reader will find enough to get a hint of David's nightmares. To Gerald, thanks for incomparable typing and patience.

I owe thanks also to the 1974-75 and 1975-76 I.S.W. (Institute of Spirituality and Worship) groups, of the Jesuit School of Theology at Berkeley, who were the patient listeners to much of this book's content via workshop conferences. Without that original "raison d'être" I would never have ventured to apply myself to this pleasant task.

I would like to thank Father Dan O'Hanlon, Father Joe Powers and Father Bob Dailey, all of the Jesuit School of Theology at Berkeley for helpful suggestions and encouragement. Likewise, Brother Tolbert McCarroll of Starcross Monastery, Annapolis, California. To Father Matthew Torpey of Holy Spirit Abbey, Conyers, Georgia, goes my gratitude for his suggestions regarding Chapters One and Two. To Dom Thomas Keating, Father William Meninger and Father Basil Pennington of St. Joseph's Abbey, Spencer, Massachusetts, my thanks for their critique and suggestions pertaining to Chapter Eight on Centering Prayer.

Archimandrite Kallistos Ware arrived on my local scene like St. Paul "as one born out of due time," so to say; and by his critique of my chapter on the Jesus Prayer, he has saved me the embarrassment of putting into print some historical inaccuracies. I am deeply grateful and indebted to him for his kindly assistance in improving this chapter and for his suggestions regarding other parts of the book.

I must express my gratitude to Dr. Mary Giles, editor of *Studia Mystica* and professor of spirituality at California State University at Sacramento, who gave me the benefit of a feminine outlook and some suggestions on how to make the text more helpful to the lay reader.

I have heeded most, but not all, of the suggestions offered to me by so many kind and encouraging hearts. To all who helped me, my sincere thanks.

Finally, to Richard Payne of Paulist Press go my special thanks for guiding this book in its last steps to publication. May it in some way glorify the God to whom we belong.

Foreword

It gives me great joy, as an Orthodox Christian, to commend this work by a Cistercian monk, my personal friend since my visit to the Abbey of New Clairvaux in the summer of 1977. Reading the pages that follow, at once there came to my mind the prophetic words of another American Cistercian, Fr. Thomas Merton: "If I can unite *in myself* the thought and the devotion of Eastern and Western Christendom, the Greek and the Latin Fathers, the Russians with the Spanish mystics, I can prepare in myself the reunion of divided Christians. From that secret and unspoken unity in myself can eventually come a visible and manifest unity of all Christians. . . . We must contain all divided worlds in ourselves and transcend them in Christ."

In *Don't You Belong to Me?* the monk of New Clairvaux has achieved precisely such an act of "containing" and "transcending." He draws first of all upon his own tradition, quoting frequently from the Cistercian writers of the twelfth and thirteenth centuries, and himself displaying much of their directness, warmth and simplicity. He draws also upon the Desert Fathers of Egypt, who are the common source of our monastic prayer life, whether we are Catholics or Orthodox. And he speaks of things that are particularly precious to Eastern Christians, such as the continual Prayer of the Heart and the Invocation of the Name of Jesus. And to all this he has added a vivid personal note of his own.

Doubtless there are things here which an Orthodox might

have expressed differently. For example, William of St. Thierry's words about the Holy Spirit, cited in Chapter Two, represent a Western rather than an Eastern approach; and most Orthodox spiritual fathers would be more reserved about "praying in tongues." But I find in this book, never contradictions or opposition between East and West, but only variations of emphasis.

Again and again, even when the author does not refer to them explicitly, I have been reminded of what our Orthodox teachers affirm. "Centering Prayer," as explained in Chapter Eight, is very close to the Jesus Prayer: and here I am especially grateful for the clear distinction which the author makes between "Centering Prayer" and TM. The Orthodox approach to Scripture reading is exactly that developed in Chapter Ten, "The Way of Lectio Divina." The Christian East, less analytical than the West, has not worked out the four steps of the "ladder" as clearly as Guigo, but our basic teaching is the same. In the words of an eighteenth-century Russian, St. Tikhon of Zadonsk, "Whenever you read the Gospel, Christ Himself is speaking to you. And while you read, you are praying and talking with Him."

This book has renewed my own sense of God's closeness and His love, and I am confident that it will do the same for many others. I shall not quickly forget the first chapter, with its moving picture of the human person as essentially rooted in God, "God-sourced." And I am so very thankful that the author is practical and specific in his directions about prayer. It is related of Thomas Carlyle as a young man how, returning from church one Sunday morning, he said to his mother with exasperation: "I cannot think why they preach such long sermons. If I were a minister, I would go up into the pulpit and say no more than this: Good people, you know what you ought to do. Now go and do it." "Yes, Thomas," replied his mother quietly, "and will you tell them *how?*"

Fortunately the author of this book tells us not only *what* but *how*.

"Prayer is the test of everything," says Bishop Theophan the Recluse. "If prayer is right, everything is right." May this book, embodying the personal experience of many years, guide its readers on the right path, encouraging them to offer living prayer to the living God.

Archimandrite Kallistos Ware
Monk of the Monastery of
St. John the Theologian
Patmos, Greece

Introduction

Bruno was dying. A long, prayerful life lay behind him. He had been in the monastery more than fifty years, spending them for the most part as guestmaster, serving the guests and visitors to the Abbey of Our Lady of the Desert near Toulouse, France. Now, in 1934, awaiting the Lord's coming with joy and love, he could hear words that had echoed many times in his heart: "But don't you belong to Me?"

When Bruno was small enough to count his age on one hand and a finger, he had an experience which rooted his whole life in God. He came of a poor and devout family. His father was a weaver of cloth and all of his large family were involved in his work, including the tiny hands of Bruno. Each evening the father would gather all of his children around him and read to them from the Bible or the Lives of the Saints.

Little Bruno was awed with the greatness and majesty of God, as his father portrayed him. God was so great and Bruno was so little. The boy was mystified. How could God love Bruno? One day when the child was preoccupied with this question, he heard an inner voice say to him: "I do love you." And he asked, "But how can you?" And the voice responded, "Do your father and mother love you?" Bruno replied, "Yes . . . but I belong to them." And the voice came back, "But don't you belong to Me?"[1]

About five years after Bruno died, another lad in another part of the world was riding home on his bike after watching his heroes, the local college nine, win the final game of their baseball season. It was a fine spring day in May and the air was mild and refreshing. The bees and the butterflies were kissing every blossom. School vacation was in sight and a carefree summer stretched ahead. Life was rosy indeed. I was thirteen at the time.

Coasting downhill from the stadium, the thought occurred to me: "What's so hard about getting to heaven? Where's the struggle?" No inner voice responded to my musing. It was the first of many painful presumptions that I can recall in my life.

Within days I began experiencing some strange sensations. There was something about them that made me uneasy and secretive, then guilty and fearful with scrupulosity. At a Saturday evening confession I had the first stirrings of sexuality explained to me by an understanding and kindly pastor.

"Well, that takes care of that!" thought I. But it didn't. Those delightful sensations kept coming and all I was assured of was, "It's OK so long as you don't give in." I was ready to climb the wall.

And then someone seemed to be present, very near, but exactly where I didn't know. But he made a big difference. I couldn't make sense out of sexuality to save me, but a helper was slowly becoming a very dear companion and personal friend, whom I blindly "talked with." It was the birth in me of a conscious and deliberate effort to pray in response to someone's helping presence. Childhood was over. Personal responsibility hit with fearful force.

For all of the blushing, tears and fears that those persistent temptations triggered off in me, I came to feel grateful to God for them to the degree that they drove me in desperation to him for assistance and consolation . . . which was the beginning of a long friendship with Christ. And by his goodness to me, I learned gradually neither to despise sexuality nor to fear it. He helped me to accept it as a great gift, a God-given gift, of creative power along with its accompanying capacity for intimate human sharing. He enabled me to appreciate its delicate richness, and even to see it revealing, analogically, something mysterious and marvelous about God's own love and communion in Tri-unity.

Why God became a personal reality to little Bruno at age five or six and to me much later at the onset of puberty is his own secret. What is important is that God has made us to "run into" him somewhere along life's journey,[2] that he might lift our life to a new level of love and joy.

Having begun this book with an account of God's unique dealings with the tiny child Bruno and an impressionable event in my adolescence, I would like to expand upon and share some of the lights that have moved my own life toward God, not, however, relating them for the most part in a personalized way.

Part One may be characterized as inspirational. Part Two is historical/traditional, which has meant much to me personally. Part Three is a little more heady, being an analysis of prayer—prayer from the perspective of an appropriately constant response to God's love and care. And, finally, Part Four is an explication of three Christian/monastic "techniques" (using the word loosely) for fostering a life of prayer.

This book may appear to the perceptive reader as being not a single book at all, but several booklets in one binding. On the other hand, as author I prefer to think that I have treated several aspects of prayer in a variety of genre, offering something to everybody interested in God and prayer. The person who is looking for a stimulus to his or her fervor will hopefully find it in the first two chapters. The analyst may find satisfaction further on, especially in Chapters Five to Seven. And the practical-minded reader who is looking for methods and ways to pray will find them in the final three chapters. Let the reader, then, dig in where he or she likes, according to his or her interests.

My hope and prayer are that the careful and reflective reader may realize ever more deeply, and with joyful gratitude, the gentle leadings of the Lord in his or her own life.

Part One

Part One, consisting of two chapters, will be a kind of "mulligan stew." It will be the sharing of things that have been simmering in my heart and consciousness for some time—things that pertain to some of the ultimates of human existence. I hope that they will add a richer meaning to the more studied and systematic chapters which will follow.

Chapter One

God's Dream for Us

Having fashioned us, God knows what is suitable for us and loves what is good for us. His gracious will for us flows from his wisdom, goodness and love; flows from a Father's caring heart.

Because of his concern God cannot bear to see us do ourselves harm by evil and sin speaking anthropomorphically and yet very truly. Because of his love he wants what is good for us as any good parent would, or what any good spouse desires from his beloved. By our seeking what is really good for us, we seek his will and wisdom *in us*. Thus he is praised and glorified and he is pleased and "kindled" in love. Indeed, our fulfilling life itself becomes his glory, because it is the life of God himself in us.

The Mysterious and Basic Question

But this only drives us back to that mysterious and most basic question: Why do we exist at all? And even more, why do I exist? Only God himself "contains" the full and real answer. And only God himself does not have to ask this question. He is his own source and fulfillment. But we ask it because we are neither our own source nor our own fulfillment. An "answer," when given, never really satisfies us, no matter how profound and how well articulated. It could be nothing more than a fine notional explanation, but the real satisfying "answer' must be a living experience hidden in Living Truth, awaited in faith for another day when God will draw us completely into his own fulfillment. The "answer" is wedded to the mystery of God's own indescribable Love-Life.

What is more important than an "answer" here and now is that we experience the inner prompting of grace and love's gratitude so that we be moved to respond intensely to God's love and the glorious "dream" he has for each of us. God "needs" our love because he wants to be loved by us, knowing that that is what will make us completely happy.[1]

God is central for us. He is central and he can't help it. That's the way things are because *He IS* and we are *of Him*. "Not one thing had its being but through him. All that came to be had life in him. . . ."[2] Thus it is he who has called us forth out of nothingness. No! Not out of nothingness. He has called us forth from his *own* existence, life, be-ing[3] . . . where we always exist for him. But now he wants us to exist for ourselves to enjoy ourselves in him, and to enjoy *him*.

With reference to all of God's creation the psalmist declares, "He spoke, and it was created; he commanded, and there it stood. Yahweh's love fills the earth."[4]

Our existence and life are his gift. His creating and conserving act mediates our existence. Never for a moment do we sustain ourselves. Either he does it or we cease, totally. There is no other way to exist. Our standing forth in reality is his gift . . . this very moment . . . the moment just past . . . the moment next to come. Each moment.

He never takes back his gift! He will never take back our existence; it is an everlasting gift! We are at the beginning, the barest beginning of our existence, and it's never going to terminate. For everlasting years our being is His gift, and not just any gift, but a gift from His own Being.[5] We shall always be in this relationship with God.

So God is truly central whether we are conscious of it or not. And certainly there are not a few people wearing out their soles on the pavement of our streets who are completely oblivious of their relationship to a God of sustaining power and love.

"Nosce te ipsum," ("Know thyself.") was a goal of the monks of the desert as well as the early Fathers of the Church and the

saints down the ages. How can we really know ourselves as we are, unless we know ourselves as God-sourced beings? We don't know ourselves as we are unless we know ourselves in this relationship with God.

Now His "sourcing" is not something poured down from heaven, but arises from within us, within us where God Himself is. On the other hand we can say that we arise within God and have our existence in Him. Nothing is or can have being outside His Being or beyond the "reach" of His Being. "Where" He is, we are. "Where" we are, He is. Where He is we are—always arising out of His existence. Where we are He is— by His creative sustaining power.

As creatures, having our source in God and our fulfillment in Him, we are assuredly finite. But if we probe beneath the surface of our activity, of our thinking, feeling, choosing, sensing, judging, and deeper yet, beyond attitudes, habits, convictions, dispositions, beyond the unconscious and the soure of all impulse and instinct and reflex, beyond everything functional in us, we come to a root, to the core of being. That core is God. No. God is at the core. God is other than the core. God is within the core, and all through the core, and beyond the core, closer to the core than the core. Yes! then there *is* something of us that is God.

Now philosophically, I suppose, such an expression could be torn to shreds. But that's all right. I could suffer that gladly in the face of the possibility of coming to that moment of glorious intuition of seeing the incredible union we have with God ... to that point where we see that we are what God is sharing with us of himself, out of his unlimited sourcing power and love.

God's creating is not other or separate from himself. God is all that he does. So, for us to be just ourselves alone is utterly impossible. God is the core of our being or we just aren't. We are more closely united with God than we can ever be united with parents or marriage partner or offspring, or friend or confrere.

Moreover, it is the rootedness in God of all of us that binds us together, that gives us an incomprehensibly close union, an incredible divine relation with one another.

What does all of this mean then but a ground and context

and motive for prayer, as an expression of love and joy. Prayer can be eager response to this relationship with our uncreated Source. It can be total, grateful, acceptance of our existence and life situation. It can be communion with Love.

Gift Upon Gift

But we have more than this basic gift, this shared gift of being. God builds gift upon gift, enriching, enhancing, bestowing life in abundance. With each gift, with each step forward, we become more than we were. We are making a journey . . . to reach a fullness. Our beginning is bound by body, space and time—to be used while transcending. While part of the Good News is "I am with you," the path is not always obvious. We find it—him—in light, shadow and night, in creation, trial and faith . . . but always pressing on to Life beyond life, no matter how abundant here.

We are *"capax Dei,"* made for total deification. We are finite expressions of his infinite self-expression. Created icons. Our inheritance was spoiled by a *"felix culpa"* only to be rewarded by the gift of gifts so that "heaven is wedded to earth and man is reconciled to God."[6] We are proclaimed the bride by the good news; made sons by adoption, sons with the Son, children of the Father. "For God took the sinless Christ and poured into him our sins. Then, in exchange, he poured God's goodness into us!"[7]

St. Paul hymns it this way:

Blessed be God the Father of our Lord Jesus Christ,
who has blessed us with all the spiritual blessings of heaven
    in Christ.
Before the world was made, he chose us, chose us in Christ,
to be holy and spotless, and to live through love in his
    presence,
determining that we should become his adopted sons,
    through
Jesus Christ for his own kind purposes,
to make us praise the glory of his grace,
his free gift to us in the Beloved,
in whom, through his blood, we gain our freedom, the
    forgiveness of our sins.

Such is the richness of the grace which he has showered on
   us
in all wisdom and insight.
He has let us know the mystery of his purpose,
the hidden plan he so kindly made in Christ from the
   beginning
to act upon when the times had run their course to the end:
that he would bring everything together under Christ as
   head,
everything in the heavens and everything on earth.
And it is in him that we were claimed as God's own,
chosen from the beginning,
under the predetermined plan of the one who guides all
   things
as he decides by his own will;
chosen to be, for his greater glory,
the people who would put their hopes on Christ before he
   came . . .
you too have been stamped with the seal of the Holy Spirit
   of Promise,
the pledge of our inheritance for those whom God has
   taken for his own,
to make his glory praised.[8]

This is our true genealogy. How the Jews were jealous of
their ancestry, treasuring their share as God's people, who
were inheritors of the promise. This was merely a human
genealogy; a descent from the man of faith, Abraham. But, the
Father has made us his own "in Christ"—a divine genealogy—
sealed by the Spirit. What reason for elation. We are his children forever, and we are brothers and sisters to one another
with the saints forever. We may rejoice for our names are
written in the Book of Life, which is the Father's heart. We
need only respond and strive to be what we are in him, in his
"dream" for us.

Contingency Glorified

Yet, when we take stock of how contingent upon innumerable conditions our very existence has been, we may feel very
insignificant, like little Bruno. We may indeed feel that we are

the result of accidental circumstances. If anything had happened to even one of our parents before our conception ...! But our situation is more terrifyingly contingent than that. We were dependent upon f-o-u-r grandparents. And eight great grandparents. Sixteen great, great grandparents.[9] By only the eighth generation our delicate dependency threads back to two hundred and fifty-six grandparents. How tenuous our existence! An accident to any of them ....! But God has us in his own genealogy, and that is enough. We are, and we are his.

Reflect, too, how fragile our everyday life is with emotional and moral ups and downs. It is not difficult for most of us to fall into periodic discouragement and even slide into occasional depression. These are the times when we feel we are not worth much, and therefore feel unwanted, anxious and lonely. This may be especially true and especially trying in the case of the person who is caught in a habit of sin with all its accompanying sense of guilt, remorse and the apparent hopelessness of falling again and again.

In the face of our sin and sinfulness, well may we wonder why so great a God treasures the likes of us. If the love of mature and good parents is an unconditional love for their children, God, their Creator, is infinitely more solicitous. God has not only mirrored his divine properties in material creation, He has also mirrored his moral attributes in the hearts of good persons: love, mercy, kindness, compassion, generosity, long-suffering, patience, tender concern, intimacy, contagious peace and joy.

Good parents are not known to reject, abandon or destroy their children when they make their appearance in the house dripping with the stinking mud from a spill in the gutter,[9a] nor even when two of them get into a squabble and start beating each other over the head and tearing out one another's hair, amid screams and childish fury. Maturity and love find a way to clean or reconcile, or otherwise set their children on a right course of calm and peaceful life again ... until the next mini-tragedy. By such prudence and indulgent love youngsters wax to adulthood with a sense of acceptance, worthwhileness and security, arriving in their turn to maturity and full capacity to love.

While a child may be anxious about his dirty condition as

he enters the house, or the squabbling children may be smarting with their nasty and guilty feelings after the fight, the parents are able to maintain a broader horizon and deeper appreciation of life. They see beyond this moment of the child's misery to the goodness of the child's being and future fullness. But so it may be with us, smarting under our most recent failure or fault, and seeing ourselves at our worst! God, with the eagle eye of eternity and infinity, beholds us undoubtedly at our best, our ultimate best. Why not? From where he stands he sees us at every moment of our life and existence: laden and imbued with all the good things he gives to us in this life and beyond. He sees us as the saints we will be when he is all in us and when we will be like him for seeing him as he is[10] ... mirroring his delightful attributes back to him. Treasure us he does because we are his, securely his, with his own likeness. We are always before him, like his uncreated Son, who has redeemed us, made us righteous, made us one with himself, engrafted and made vitally one with him.[11] In fact, the Father never sees us apart from his Son. Seeing the Son, he lovingly beholds head and members together. He has never seen us any other way. Never one without the other. Such we have been, are now, and ever will be eternally present to the Father and beautiful to behold by him.

Trusting Love

Glancing back for a moment for the sake of tying things together, we noticed that "knowing ourselves" involves knowing ourselves as God-sourced-beings. But it involves also realizing the greatness of God and his loving generosity toward us, in conjunction with our creatureliness and fragility. The love of God attracts and draws us to him and our lowliness and neediness urge and push us toward him. The outgrowth of these two thrusts is prayer of praise, thanksgiving, admiration, appreciation, complemented by petition and supplication.

Now, the more we are able to open ourselves to so majestic a God and to accept our own neediness with childlike simplicity, the more we will thrive, expand and jubilate. This innocent trusting is so important. To trust him and to let go.

The following incident may help to illustrate this. During

World War II (the epiphany of distrust) while the massive incineration of life rained from high-flying bombers and rockets upon the cities of England and Germany and elsewhere, a captivating account came my way of the rescue of a little boy from a burning home in a place far removed from the carnage of war. A father returned home one evening to find flames glowing in the windows of his home. His wife and daughter were running down the steps as he approached, but his little son was trapped upstairs in a bedroom. As the father came around to the side of the house, the youngster was leaning over the sill with the flames behind him and the smoke pouring out of the window. The father called up to him; "Jump, Jimmy! I'll catch you!" But the boy replied "Dad, I can't see you!" "That's all right," cried the father, "I can see you. JUMP!" The boy climbed onto the sill, pitched himself into the air, and plummeted into the strong arms of his father.

Trust in his father saved him from a burning death; trust also enabled him to overcome the fear of being shattered on the sidewalk below. Who knows how much more father and son meant to each other ever after? The threat of love's loss for the one and rescue for the other shaped a mutual fondness and intimacy that later recountings could only fuel, and adorn with laughs and celebration. The goodness and enjoyableness of each incites and moves the other, and so their lives are enriched and fulfilled.

But none of this could be if the boy had not been willing to die the death of following his feelings and his will to hold onto the sill instead of following the words and the will of his father. Because he let go, he would know the mingled joys and adventure of familial love.

Out of God's love we have come-to-be specifically for the adventurous divine encounters that trust makes possible. Trusting and receiving beget further trust and an ever deepening love affair with God. Prayer flames up. It is the conversation of love. Prayer is the language of word and the language of attitude spoken in every situation of life: a sorrowing love, contrite, and yearning to repair a wound; a grateful love, expressing gratitude for help in need and for every good thing, or just gratitude that the Beloved is; and sometimes ecstatic love. Prayer becomes heart abiding in heart.

Before hastening on, let us eye a common concrete difficulty, coming at it by way of two contrasting incidents.

Recently, when I was walking to a Greyhound Bus station to return to New Clairvaux, I witnessed what was for me a depressing scene. Coming down a residential side street, I noticed several children playing on a front porch across the street. Before I passed, a car pulled up and a burly fellow emerged and headed toward the steps as a child—perhaps four years old—came down to meet him. "Why all the noise?" he shouted at her and he stomped up the steps and disappeared through the door, leaving the tot standing there, pensive and subdued by his cold rebuke.

As I continued on my way another scene passed through my mind. It was years ago, before I left home to enter religious life. The next door neighbor would pull in the driveway and his three little children would often be playing in the yard. Before he had time even to get out, they would be at the side of the car, and as he stepped out they would joyously surround him and he would go down on one knee and gather them all into his arms and hug them. And then the happy procession would proceed to the back door with gleeful shouts of "Daddy is home!"

If the children of these two scenes were grounded in their mode of experiencing their heavenly Father through the way they experienced the love of their earthly fathers, the first child is obviously going to experience God in a different way than the children of the next door neighbor. While the great problem and stumbling block for a child raised in a non-religious home may be faith, for a child reared in a so-called religious but insecure and parentally cold, harsh and quarrelsome home it will probably be trust in a heavenly Father. Should it surprise us then that many of us in today's world suffer a difficulty with faith or trust? Defenses and coping-devices (self-defeating as they may be) for clinging to some sense of security and self-worth have taken root in us from childhood. We are not able to abandon them the moment we recognize that our life will blossom if we only stride forward with strong faith and trust in God. Much patience and prayerful meditation will be necessary to dampen our acquired tendency to hang on to our inadequate substitutes for true religious response. But where there is a will there is a way and God is with us to help us. We are never alone. And our success is fatherly joy and triumph for him. So here we are, back to God's sheer goodness and our response of prayer.

St. Bernard has provided us with an exquisite passage which portrays us in our wayward propensities and inconsistencies, while revealing something beautiful about God. It goes like this: God made men, and he wanted men to be happy. And he saw that they couldn't be happy unless they were good. So God told them to be good. And then God looked and he saw that they weren't good. They were envious and jealous and ambitious, and so they hated one another and killed one another and they were wretched. And so God bethought himself and said, "That creature of mine, man, what can I do to make him good and so make him happy? If I take away his free will, I will only have a donkey or an animal that won't freely serve me and love me. That's no good. What else can I do? Well, that creature of mine is frightened of pain and suffering; if I *threaten* him with everlasting pain and darkness and separation from all that is beautiful and good, perhaps he will be brought to goodness and so to happiness." And God threatened man even with the eternal torment of everlasting punishment. And then God looked and saw that not so were men brought to goodness. And so God thought a second time. And he said, "That creature of mine, man, is not only frightened of suffering and pain, but he loves enjoyment and he loves above all things LIFE. He loves to live. And so, if I promise him an eternal bliss and happiness and life with me, he may be brought to goodness and so to happiness." So God promised them eternal life in union with himself. And he looked and saw that not even so were men brought to goodness. They were still wicked. In spite of threats and in spite of promises! And so God scratched his head, and he said, "This creature of mine, he's not only frightened of pain and suffering, he not only loves enjoyment and life, but he is an affectionate creature. He loves to love. And he loves to be loved. And so if I really prove to him that I love him, he may be drawn to goodness and so to happiness. If I become a baby, he may love me from that tenderness which people feel towards a baby. If he sees me in agony and dying, through sheer compassion he may love me." And so God became man and was an infant and died on the cross for us. And then God said, "What more could I have done for my vineyard that I have not done?"[12]

Truly, what more could he have done? If we are not moved to respond to such goodness, what will move us?[13]

Perspective

Let us circle back now for another look at God's majesty and our significant insignificance.

Two extremes confuse and confront us about our material universe: some things are too small to see and others are too big to apprehend. Smaller bodies keep showing up in bigger micro-scopes and more distant masses keep twinkling in better tele-scopes. Maxi-scopic numbers compound the confusion. I sup-pose most of us moderns can recall some of our high school studies in general science or particular sciences. Our own bodies are claimed to be a mass of a quadrillion little cells (give or take a few depending on belt spread and height); and each cell is a complex of smaller molecules of organic compounds, and these composed of atoms, and atoms of neutrons, protons and electrons, and where we eventually stop nobody knows. The human eye is small enough, but there are twenty million nerve endings in the retina alone. We carry around about thirty-five million gastric glands in our stomachs, with five billion red blood cells swimming around in each cubic centi-meter of our blood.

Going in the other direction, our globe is about 8,000 miles to jog through from one side to the other; and the sun is 864,000 miles across, capable of containing about 1,300,000 or more earths within. As we gallop around the sun at 66,600 mph, the sun is careening off in the direction of the star Vega at a speed of 43,000 mph—but we need fear no collision since by the time we get there, one million years will have passed and Vega will be elsewhere. Ole Betelguese surpasses our sun in diameter a thousand times, having a girth that could enclose our sun and all of our planets in their vast orbits out as far as Mars. Sirius, the "dog star" is 52 trillion miles away (9 light years) and has 26 times the luminous power of our sun; the distance is appreciated since if it ever replaced our sun, all of our oceans, lakes and rivers would boil away and we would be steamed to death. Rigel has 21 thousand times the luminous power of our sun and is a fortunate 544 light years away. Canopus is 91 thousand times and further away yet. Stars of course vary also in size and density. Sirius' companion star is about the size of our earth and has a density of over 200 tons per cubic inch. Perish the thought of being struck by a cubic inch of such a small star!

So far we have only been considering individual bodies. Our visible star neighbors form one Star Cluster which is a mere crumb of the Milky Way, which is our particular galactic system of star clusters. Our galaxy is said to have a diameter of six hundred quadrillion miles. Now there happen to be millions of other such galaxies swirling around God's universe with elbow room of unimaginable distances.[14]

One thing that is clear from the foregoing is that bodily, we are of insignificant size compared with the enormous masses of the cosmos. And so is God—which requires further comment.

If we inadvertently have the habit of imagining God as co-extensive with his created universe, so that we think of him extending as far out as the most distant stars and galaxies, we are going to suffer from a capricious stretch that fails to appreciate both our universe's diffused insignifance as well as the real marvel of God's immensity.

Almost any child who lays hands on binoculars is delighted to look at things now through one end of the "toy" and then through the other, tickled by seeing the same things enlarged at one end and shriveled at the other. Now if our whole universe, which seems so immense *to us*, began a gradual and unperceived contraction—all things and we being maintained in their present spacial relationships—what now seems absolutely huge might shrink to the size of a wee fragile hazelnut[15] which you can cradle in the cup of your hand.

Let us suppose this fanciful phenomenon happened to all except the reader. You have escaped the universal shrinkage, and you hold in your hand this tiny world of beings. They aren't aware of any change and everything goes on as before.

Well might the words of Wisdom apply, "In your sight the whole world is like a grain of dust that does not even tip the scales; like a drop of morning dew falling to the ground."[16]

Now look for the astronauts sweeping around their miniscopic orbits or at the Russian cosmonaut scanning infinitesimal space for the existence of God! Notice the victors panting on the summit of bump Everest. See the money changer at his desk enmeshed in his somber counting, and other men at other minutiae. And don't fail to observe the parish priest and the assembled faithful gathered in their place of worship, lifting up the fragment of bread and the chalice of wine. They receive from the Father, in return, Infinity made finite for the sake of his creatures, come as the Son of Man to serve in insignificance, come that they may have life in his abundant immensity. By that union and that communion they breathe with his transcendent life and enchant the Father who sees his Son in all and knows them as his own children.

Reduce the cosmos to a submicroscopic parvitude and expand it to a supertelescopic amplitude. Does it make any difference? God's immensity is another dimension. God's immensity is uncreated Spirit and absolute being. Space is created relativity which for God is neither large nor small.

But God constituted *us* more than bodies and breathed into us living spirits. As we look out from our small stature beyond the horizons of space and time, to another dimension transcending extension and succession, we are able to behold with God something of his dream for us. We can know that our present "imprisonment" in space and body is a passing moment preparing for something greater ... spirits freed in the universe. Yes, and more. Re-embodied spirits standing within the immensity of God; finitude set free in the immensity of infinite Spirit; created life taken into the warmth, the life, the love of the infinite Son, forever.

Sharing God's dream is quickening to prayer, which helps us to realize that love can never be satisfied with partial gifts or part of the beloved. Anyone who has truly and deeply loved another knows that love reaches out to take full possession of the beloved, while making a complete and interminable gift of self. God reaches out to take possession of our spirit, first by grace and then by death. But not being satisfied with less than all that we beautifully are, excepting our sins alone, he will re-embody us with the risen glories of the Son, that we may stroll arm in arm with the beloved on the crystal sea of the New Jerusalem.

Do most of us live dreadfully short of perspective in this present life? After millions of years (if you'll pardon the limitations of the expression) on our mystical honeymoon, and as we are gathered around the banquet table I suppose we will look back to the moment of years we spent on earth and talk over old times. We will muse together over our myopia and monochromism, and laugh at how much ado we could make over nothing. And the honeymoon?—billions of years later it will ever have its beginning freshness of mutual possession and bliss of life and love. No end in sight. Indeed, no end!

Chapter Two

Guide Me in the Way
That is Everlasting

Come down to earth again. Until God's "dream" finds this fulfillment in us, we have his work of salvation to take in hand for ourselves and for others, the family of God on earth. We might see it succinctly through the eyes and experience of St. Paul.[1] St. Paul met the resurrected and victorious Christ.[2] Through his first encounters and those that soon followed,[3] he was getting the message. Christ is, and Jesus of Nazareth lives; he is moving creation to a goal—from darkness to light, through faith and forgiveness to the promised inheritance.[4] Paul experienced the need of *metanoia* and began to preach it to Jews and pagans alike.[5] He had personal experience of the life and power of Christ working in him and also through him in behalf of others as the book of Acts displays profusely. Nor did *metanoia* have to be accomplished all by oneself, by keeping the Law or by any other exterior thing, but by the Spirit of Christ, given to man, working in his heart by the power of many gifts of sanctification and service.[6] The same Spirit of God binds all sublimely and efficaciously together to be Christ's body, church, bride.[7] "In this way we are all to come to unity in our faith and in our knowledge of the Son of God, until we become the perfect man, fully mature with the fullness of Christ himself."[8] *Metanoia* becomes death to the selfish self.[9] "All baptized in Christ, you have all clothed yourselves in Christ."[10] Like Paul and with Paul we can all say, "Now I can live for God. I

have been crucified with Christ, and I live now not with my
own life but with the life of Christ who lives in me."[11] The
new Adam by the power of his Spirit working in us makes us a
new creature, one single New Man,[12] being made ready for the
age to come. "We are God's work of art, created in Christ Jesus
to live the good life as from the beginning he had meant us to
live it."[13] And so, Christ bears us with him as he goes to the
Father, to dwell in the Father's bosom. "God loved us with so
much love that he ... brought us to life with Christ Jesus ...
and raised us up with him and gave us a place with him in
heaven, in Christ Jesus."[14] We live as sons with the Son. "The
spirit you received ... is the spirit of sons, and it makes us cry
out, Abba, Father!"[15] "So we shall stay with the Lord for ever.
With such thoughts as these you should comfort one another."[16] "... And for all things give thanks to God."[17]

Such is the Paschal Mystery: Christ, sent from the Father,
living among us, dying and rising for us, and taking us with
him back to the bosom of the Father, sharing with us his
incorruptibility and immortality. How fitting then to live a life
of prayer that engages and immerses us in a love response to
the kindness of the Father, Son and Holy Spirit. Our life in
Christ and Christ's in us is a life of love/prayer; and prayer is
the dwelling in and the welling over of our love life.

Deifying Indwelling

What is implicit and even explicit in many of the texts of
St. Paul above is the indwelling presence of God in our very
being. But if we want the most profound declarations of this
consoling mystery, we must turn to St. John. At the com-
mencement of Chapter I we pondered the "necessary" indwelling presence of God; necessary, since our very being cannot
exist aside from God and he is the core and root-source of our
very existence, so that we are whatever he shares with us of
himself, by his sourcing power.

Now we want to consider that complementary indwelling
which is promised in the Scriptures, found especially in those
awesome and sweet assurances of Christ to the disciples as he
prepared them for his departure to the Father.

After Jesus manifested how complete was his love for his apostles by cleansing their dusty feet, he sat them down at table and spoke to them His message of love. "If you love me you will keep my commandments . . . and the Father will give you another Advocate to be with you for ever . . . he is with you, he is in you."[18] And then Jesus promises and includes himself and our Father: "You will understand that I am in my Father and you in me and I in you . . . and my Father will love him, and we shall come to him and make our home with him."[19]

This indwelling is that Divine Presence which floods our human existence with a transcendent fullness, sweeping our being and life up to the exalted plane of God's own inner love life. Our natural life is deified, drawn into and incorporated in the life of the Trinity. And this is the sublime difference between God's "necessary" indwelling and his deifying indwelling.

Jesus declared, "My own peace I give you, a peace the world cannot give, this is my gift to you."[20] "The peace I give you isn't fragile like the peace the world gives" is the way another translator expresses it;[21] and it certainly isn't! It is the assurance, not of human inanities, but of divine realities engaging the Mystery of Life Itself. I am with you . . . in you . . . you live by my life! . . . I will take you where I am . . . you will share my glory, which is the Father's own glory.[22]

Jesus tells the apostles, "I have told you this so that my own joy may be in you and your joy may be complete."[23] He had to tell them this because the divine indwelling like that necessary presence rooted in our nature is not all that obvious to us. These two causes of joy will be fully clear and realized by us only when we have been taken up in glory. Jesus went on to describe how the apostles would experience the sense of his loss, the sense of his absence, and that they would taste sorrow and sadness like unto that of a woman suffering the pains of childbirth.[24]

And then there is an ecclesial dimension to the divine indwelling which we should not pass over. In fact it is part of the teleology of this mystery. "I have given them the glory you gave to me, that they may be one as we are one. With me in them and you in me, may they be so completely one . . ."[25] And

he adds, "I have loved them as much as you loved me. Father, I
want those you have given me to be with me where I am, so
that they may always see the glory you have given me . . ."[26] It
is the *ecclesia*, the body of Christ, fashioned on earth by Christ's
love and fulfilled in heaven in his own glory.

St. Paul helps us to understand a little of what our glory in
Christ will be, as well as the exquisite nature of divine indwelling. "But anyone who is joined to the Lord is one spirit with
him."[27]

A number of saints and mystics moved with love and joy
have tried to give meaning to this expression of "one spirit."
William of St. Thierry offers the following:[28]

> And as happens in the kisses of lovers, who by certain
> sweet, mutual exchange, impart their spirit each to the
> other, so the created spirit pours itself out wholly into the
> Spirit, who creates it for this very effusion; and the Creator
> Spirit infuses himself into it as he wills, and man becomes
> one spirit with God.[29]

From this figurative approach taken from William's commentary on the great nuptial poem of the Old Testament, we
see him becoming more explicit in his mystical "letter" to the
Carthusians:

> But "unity of spirit" with God for the man who has his
> heart raised on high is the term of the will's progress
> toward God. No longer does it merely desire what God
> desires, not only does it love him, but it is perfect in its love,
> so that it can will only what God wills.

> Now to will what God wills is already to be like God, to be
> able to will only what God wills is already to be what God
> is; for him to will and to be are the same thing. Therefore, it
> is well said that we shall see him fully as he is when we are
> like him, that is when we are what he is. For those who
> have been enabled to become sons of God have been en-
> abled to become not indeed God, but what God is: holy, and
> in the future, fully happy as God is. And the source of their
> present holiness and their future happiness is none other
> than God himself who is at once their holiness and their
> happiness.[30]

William now hones-in with an intensely beautiful insight into our relationship with the Holy Spirit, as we stand midway with mutual Love between Father and Son.

> [Unity of spirit] makes man one with God, one spirit, not only with the unity which comes of willing the same thing but with a greater fullness of virtue, as has been said: the inability to will anything else.
>
> It is called unity of spirit not only because the Holy Spirit brings it about or inclines a man's spirit to it, but because it is the Holy Spirit himself, the God who is Charity. He who is the Love of Father and Son, their Unity, Sweetness, Good, Kiss, Embrace and whatever else they have in common in that supreme unity of truth and truth of unity, becomes for man in regard to God in the manner appropriate to him what he is for the Son in regard to the Father or for the Father in regard to the Son through unity of substance. The soul in its happiness finds itself standing midway in the Embrace and the Kiss of Father and Son.[31]

It seems to me that to be one spirit with so good a Father and Savior and bridegroom as even to be unable to do anything but what delightfully please them is exquisite joy indeed. And to be a mutual gift, with the Holy Spirit, whom Father and Son give to each other! . . . no less happiness. Being one spirit, we are thus taken into the very midst of the intimate love-life of our Triune God.

As such, and permeated with God's love and holiness, and full of risen glory from Christ, we will be anything but a lifeless gift or an empty gift, or even a passive gift. But an active gift. As the Father's created finite gift to the Son, we will really love the Son with the Father in the Holy Spirit. And as the Son's deified, risen and glorified gift restored to the Father, we will love the Father with the Son in the one same Love. We will stand with the Spirit as gift, love and joy, in the bosom of the Father and the Son.

"I will Show Myself . . ."

Recall that we saw how Jesus had to tell the apostles about the indwelling presence of God because it is a reality that is not all that obvious. The apostles would gradually grow from a knowledge about the reality of God's presence to a living sense, an awareness, a consciousness of that presence, as an intimate, loving companionship, full of spontaneity, joy and enthusiasm!

Response to God, for most of us, begins in primitive faith and petitionary prayer. God seems nebulous, aloof and almost impersonal. However as a good gardener God cultivates the tiny seed of life, and brings us to stalk, to leaf and blossom, and only later to full sweet fruit ... which is what He also did with the apostles. As our response to his love unfolds in good will, he cooperates, instigates, integrates, weeds and rakes us along in progress to a spiritual maturing, all the while revealing himself to us in ever more explicit and personal ways. Eventually we too make the joyous leap from a knowledge of God's presence, exterior and interior, to a vibrant sense of his presence, developing into an intimate friendship and loving companionship!

How did Jesus put it; what did he tell us? "Anybody who receives my commandments and keeps them will be one who loves me; and anybody who loves me will be loved by my Father, and I will love him and *show myself to him.*"[32]

In his love for us, he will show himself, disclose himself, reveal himself, manifest himself, make himself known to us, for our benefit, our comfort, our enjoyment. Now this showing, this personal epiphany has various intensities and modalities. The most physical expression of Christ's personal self-revelation to his Christian disciples down the ages has been by way of apparitions. The most hidden and much more common expression has been called, in more recent ages, *infused prayer*. And it is this latter that we want to take a peek at in a moment. Why? Because it is a powerful inducement to sacrifice all for Christ, whether we are still growing toward this encounter or have begun to experience God in this way. Secondly, it gradually becomes the deepest, richest love expression of unceasing prayer. And thirdly, having tasted the Lord and found him so sweet,[33] we become blessedly addicted to him here and forever! Making Christ primary, working toward unceasing prayer, being sweetly addicted to the Lord of love—what could be a better preparation for that startling moment after death when we will be swept up in the great arms of God to be his children, his friends, the companions of his inner life?

When Jesus reveals himself to us, he is preparing us for the revelation of the Father, here and hereafter. Indeed, in showing us himself he is showing us the Father, who has the same love for us, who is the same infinite goodness and kindness with the same attractive attributes. As he told Philip, "To have seen me is to have seen the Father, so how can you say, 'Let us see the Father?' "[34]

Jesus will come to us in this exquisite way only when it will be a help to us, and not a harm; when it will draw us intimately closer to him, and not pose a barrier, through some immature disposition on our part. His self-revelation requires a certain growth in humility, simplicity and openness to receive him, without fostering in us an ego-centering gaze, conceit, vanity, presumption, impetuosity and spiritual gluttony. To make a poor comparison, rich red and golden fruit is the glory of the apple tree, and if the tree were human it would rejoice over this glory. But for a tiny seed that springs up, and bears the glory of an apple the first year, the strain would be too much, and the struggling plant would cry out, "My glory, you are destroying me!"

Overview

In view of this difficulty let us review the "spiritual life" in broad terms to see better where infused prayer fits in. Our spiritual maturing is a growth in knowing and loving God, and for many of us it is a struggle from moral remissness to a mature childlike innocence. We see that we are moving from sin to holiness, enslavement to freedom, fragmentation to wholeness, from multiplicity to simplicity, from a certain duplicity to singleness of heart, from an instability of character and personality to balance and stability, and from a distracting busyness and insensitivity to the Holy Spirit to a peaceful and attentive sensitivity to the Holy Spirit working within us. In contemporary language[35] we may express this also as a withering of our pleasure-loving, bio-sensual, sentimental and romantic self, along with our manipulating, functional, empirical, ego self, at least insofar as these "selves" distort and disorder our true and full humanization. In contrast, the deep self, the spiritual self evolves and expands and eventually reaches the ultimate self, that self which God sees, enthroned in his heart.

Morally speaking, we try to rise from sinful ways and attachment or addiction to the "goods of the earth" by the grace of conversion. Fed by the consolations of God, we struggle with "beginner's fervor" to detach ourselves from the goods of earth and attach ourselves to the "goods of heaven," the consolations of God. When detachment from worldly ways and deliberate sin is achieved, it is then necessary to be weaned from spiritual gluttony and attachment to the spiritual milk bottle. This detachment is eventually followed by attachment to God himself and a growing freedom from the imperfections arising from our sensible appetites. This in turn is followed by a strengthening attachment to God and a freeing from imperfections arising from our spiritual aspirations to which there may have been lingering esteem and attachment, more unconscious than conscious. Thus the way is open for that complete deification which St. Teresa calls *mystical marriage* and St. John of the Cross calls *transforming union*, as well as *mystical marriage*.

Psychologically speaking, this progress may be described as a movement from a condition of hating God, or indifference to God, or fearfulness of God through a repentant, tearful conversion experience to a condition of felt love and emotional fervor, with a budding self-deception of loving God immensely and unselfishly. This is followed by periods of emotional "dryness," bringing in its wake discouragement, even depression, loneliness, and a budding deception of not loving God at all, with a painful sense of well-merited desertion by God. This in turn is followed by the joyful sense of God's "return," a renewed fervor, a growing feeling of being desired and treasured by God, with a consequent enhanced sense of self-worth and self-acceptance ... all of which are very psychologically therapeutic, advancing our emotional balance and self-possession. Further periods of aridity may follow, accompanied by a sense of being alone, but not lonely, and without losing the emotional stability and other therapeutic gains established previously. Rather they are put to the test and rooted deeply. Gradually great inner peace, constancy and confidence in God takes complete and joyful possession of us.

Prayerfully speaking, we experience an evolution in the ways we converse or communicate with God. Early in life our prayer is primarily vocal until we learn or are interiorly drawn to meditation. Meditation, and even vocal prayer, usually lead into emotionally affective outpourings of the heart. Gradually a quieter and almost wordless prayer becomes our attraction; this is a kind of silent searching of the heart, often accompanied by a vague, elusive, intangible sense of God's nearness or presence. This gives way to periods of aridity, with a sense of God's absence; and this is the subtle, hidden beginning of *infused* prayer for St. John of the Cross. What is God graciously but painfully doing but emptying out the heart and making us ready to be his true spiritual temple where he may establish himself in unity of spirit with his children. When this work is accomplished, then comes the great experience that Jesus promised, "*I will love him* and *show myself to him*."[36] The experience is never forgotten. It is intimate, vivid, consoling, joyous, full of God's overwhelming goodness and love. It may be repeated many times, varied, intensified. Creation is seen more with the eye and mind of God and his creating purpose. God shares the knowledge of his attractive and adorable attributes. Son and Spirit and Father "come." These infrequent or frequent "visits" are interspersed with periods of quiet, prolonged, interiorly attentive contemplation; a listening of the heart to an abiding love enthroned in the temple of his own making. Love may whisper, love may touch, caress, kiss or embrace; arouse purest devotion, fidelity, courage, confidence, fraternal love and every other virtue. This is infused prayer, infused love!

Let us finish the evolution of prayer-now-become-love. Is it necessary to say that God is not bestowing these intimate experiences for the sake of entertaining his followers? Nor is he just raising us to a higher plane than other men. Rather his purpose is to purify and deify us to make us one spirit with him in a consummate union of love, a love that reaches out to all others in full universality. As he is achieving this union with himself, he is also inviting us into a deeper participation in his work of redemptive love and service. No wonder then that as we share his intimacy, like the apostles and martyrs, we enter into the mystery of his suffering and humiliation. Illnesses, unusually severe temptations and other afflictions become a part of this companionship. St. Paul indicates the direction of this union,

> In your minds you must be the same as Christ Jesus: His state was divine, yet he did not cling to his equality with God but emptied himself to assume the condition of a slave, and became as men are; and being as all men are, he was humbler yet, even to accepting death, death on a cross.[37]

St. Paul does not fail to add that the Father raised Jesus on high, to the Father's glory. And of course that is what he has in mind for us too, but only after our work is finished here.

Along with sickness and other hardships, the Lord gradually withdraws the sense of his presence and infuses a sense of his absence again. This absence is eventually perceived as a subtle and real presence. And finally in the transforming union of the mystical marriage the sense of loving presence returns and abides unceasingly unless God withdraws for some special reason known to himself alone.

We Receive Him—He Receives us

This growth in prayer has its greatest and constant support for the Catholic Christian in the Sacrament of Christ's living presence, the Eucharist. The Eucharist's embodiment of all of the mysteries of God's saving action in our behalf, through the annual portrayal of the liturgical cycle of celebrations, reminds us of God's unceasing solicitude for us as a community and as individuals. More exquisite yet is the daily invitation to be incorporated into the redeeming sacrifice of Jesus and to receive the gift of himself, according to his own Gospel promise, in personal communion.[38]

Reflecting on the invariable elements of every eucharistic celebration which follow the confrontation and challenge of the Liturgy of the Word, we become aware of a dramatic and vital divine-human exchange. After the priest receives the people's gifts of bread and wine, he raises up the plate and cup in a symbolic gesture of offering. The children of God offer to their Father gifts of the earth, part of the Father's own creation ... in fact, offering to him what was his material gift to us in the first place! The marvel is that the Father not only receives these things but in his love he gives them back enchanced and transformed in the incredible Gift of his only-begotten Son, renewing, continuing Bethlehem in our midst.

But before the Father gives us this Gift, there is an interval of prayer which, as priests and people of God, we want to mean: "Father, receive *us* too, with our gifts; make us pleasing to your heart and worthy of what you are going to do for us." Celebrant and assembly alternate in thanksgiving and praise of God's goodness, and then become attentive as the Spirit of his love gives us our redeemer, living and real, in our presence. And then it happens, finite gifts offered, received, and graciously given back as an infinite gift.

And what do we do with this great gift? We turn around once more and ask our Father to receive his Son ... receive his suffering, death, resurrection and indescribable love—for our well-being. We don't neglect to join our lives with his, our sacrifice with his universal sacrifice.

The Father takes us all into his embrace for we are become identified with Jesus. Our incorporation in Christ and our bond of unity among ourselves must be made manifest there and then. The Father gives us his Gift, makes him present in our midst, not just to look at but to take to ourselves in consummated love and commitment. We receive life and light to destroy our death and darkness. In that moment we are made ready for Eternal Life, for that very union for which we were especially created. The Paschal Mystery coming to reality!

But we don't pass over the boundary of our present life at this sublime moment. We carry this mystery of love into every part of our temporal life. We learn to share God's love with each other; we learn to support one another in burden and prayer, activating God's call within us to step from this life to a richer one at his fulfilling moment.

Also involved here is the three-fold movement of Holy

Communion: from desire, to fulfillment, to beyond-death-completion. We advance from desire for this living union with Jesus—many times expressing it in prayer, sometimes enjoying the experience of his presence—to physical contact with him. Thus "spiritual communion" leads us to satisfy our longing love with his nourishing reception. God-enfleshed enters our flesh. God-enfleshed consecrates, deifies, our fleshly existence with his personal human-divine presence.

Mutual love yearns for enduring union and abiding presence—full, face to face, in a lasting embrace. Thus the "Holy Communion of death." In life Jesus offers himself to us in trust and love, and we receive him over and over in confirming, welcoming love. At death we cease to have a body in our control to receive him. He now receives us. Our bodies cease to be his temple, his bridechamber. Now it is his moment to welcome us completely into himself, to make us an everlasting part of his risen self . . .[39] that we might know the Communion of his body, the fruit of his Love, the life of his being, the bosom of the Father, and the joy of his Spirit. For this we were created. Nothing less!

Our life's journey begins from the "point" of nonexistence, passing through a few months of oblivion, born utterly helpless and totally dependent; we discover God as we mature both physically and spiritually. Death's journey seems to be a return to nothingness, whereas it is really a moment of emergence and a second birth to a fuller life. Interestingly, we are as helpless and dependent as at our birth. We don't know where to go or how to negotiate it. To submit is all we can do; let go; let it happen to us. Children do not clutch fearfully or greedily to life in the womb (would they, if they could?) but emerge to live the life they are meant to enjoy. Likewise it is neither good nor suitable for us to cling anxiously and desperately to life on earth. But just as there were loving arms and a family awaiting us the first time, there is a loving heart and a family to sweep us up into their life and light the second time.

Let us close this chapter with something of the wonderment and supplication of the Psalmist:

> It was you who created my inmost self,
> and put me together in my mother's womb;

for all these mysteries I thank you:
for the wonder of myself, for the wonder of your works.

You know me through and through,
from having watched my bones take shape
when I was being formed in secret,
knitted together in the limbo of the womb.

God, how hard it is to grasp your thoughts!
How impossible to count them!
I could no more count them than I could the sand,
and suppose I could, you would still be with me.

Make sure I do not follow pernicious ways,
and guide me in the way that is everlasting.[40]

Part Two

The Response of Prayer

"I have come so that they may have life and have it to the full."[1] Christians have been called by Christ in a personal way, at great cost to Christ himself, to live in close union with God and to receive the fullness of eternal life.[2] "The sheep hear his voice, one by one he calls his own sheep and leads them out . . . he goes ahead of them, and the sheep follow because they know his voice."[3]

We recognize his call; we respond. Prayer is a part of that response; in fact, prayer has a way of incorporating all of our response—word, work and love. It is in prayer that everything in our life can become integrated and take on its richest meaning, until eventually our whole life is a prayer and prayer is our life.

In this part we are going to focus on unceasing prayer, incessant prayer, constant prayer, continual prayer. (These are the various terms that spiritual writers use for this human-divine achievement.)

We will begin with the scriptural foundation for unceasing prayer, considering two principal texts: 1 Thessalonians 5:17 and Luke 18:1. Then, in the following chapter we will look briefly at the teaching of some of the early writers of the Church on unceasing prayer.

Chapter Three

Scriptural Foundation
for Unceasing Prayer

When St. Paul wrote to the Thessalonians, he urged them to pray unceasingly, *adialeiptōs proseuchesthe*.[1] In view of the second coming of Christ he exhorted them to:

always rejoice	*pantote chairete*
unceasingly pray	*adialeiptōs proseuchesthe*
in everything give thanks	*en panti eucharisteite*
the spirit do not quench	*to pneuma mē sheneute*[2]

This is like saying: Be happy in your faith-life. Pray without giving up. Be grateful for everything, and thus you will be working out the Father's will. Let the Spirit live in you. Let the Spirit fructify your life.

Does this text actually mean pray always in the apparent sense of a continuous flow of formal prayers? Rather I take the sense of it to be that we are not to give up prayer during our life; we are to be persevering, persistent. Turning to another part of the Scriptures, we find some of the psalms expressing this sense of persistence especially the cluster at the end of the psalter, 145 to 150 (Hebrew enumeration). In Psalm 146 the psalmist cries out:

> Praise Yahweh, my soul!
> I mean to praise Yahweh all my life,
> I mean to sing to my God as long as I live.[3]

37

He then goes on to relate how Yahweh helps and protects those
who lean on him.

Since St. Paul links prayer with rejoicing and thanksgiving, he is furthermore really aiming at a very deep, rich attitude of heart, which finds us appreciating our life and being
filled with gratitude for all that God has given us, not forgetting the prospect, the expectation of eternal life! (We will be
concerned throughout Parts II and III with these dispositions
of heart in their relationship to constant prayer.)

In Psalm 145 the psalmist is focused more directly on his
heartfelt wonder of Yahweh himself:

> I sing your praises, God my King
> I bless your name for ever and ever,
>   blessing you day after day,
> and praising your name for ever and ever.
> Can anyone measure the magnificence
> of Yahweh the great, and his inexpressible
>   grandeur?
>
> Celebrating your acts of power,
> one age shall praise your doings to another.
> Oh, the splendour of your glory, your renown!
> I tell myself the story of your marvelous deeds.[4]

Consider now our second New Testament text. Luke 18:1
tells us to pray always, *pantote proseuchesthai*, and not to faint, *kai
mē ekkakein*.[5] I like to view this text in the light of the passage
which precedes it, which concerns the "Day" of the Son of
Man (Lk. 17:22-37). Luke has Jesus telling the disciples that the
time will come when they will long to see him but cannot.
What should they do? They should not try to preserve their
lives amid the trial to come, but to let go. Be faithful to prayer,
pray constantly, and don't lose heart. The text thus bespeaks
fidelity, perseverance and trust that things will work out since
all is in the hands, the mighty hands of the Lord.

But we can and should also consider Luke 18:1 in the light
of the passage that follows it, verses 2-8, which is the parable of
the unjust judge. A cold-hearted judge is pitted against a relent-
less widow who wears[6] him down with her beseeching until he

gives way, takes up her case and sees that justice is done in her behalf. If a poor widow can get justice from such a man, will not God come to the aid of his very own who cry to him, even though he seems to delay? Again the message is persistence, perseverance and confidence in being heard and helped.[7]

A point worth noting is that specific texts mentioning unceasing prayer, while helpful, are not really the best source for grounding unceasing prayer in the deep rich sense that will unfold in the following chapters. Rather, much more light is gathered on the subject by considering the living examples that are presented to us in the Scriptures. (Treated briefly in the next chapter.)

Chapter Four

Early Fathers on Unceasing Prayer

This chapter will serve to remind us that the practice of incessant prayer is neither a novel exercise nor a contemporary art. It is a practice which has a long tradition, and lies at the very heart of Christian spirituality. We find the early Fathers of the Church, including the "Desert Fathers," speaking about it and living it out in their lives in their own special ways. It will be unnecessary for us—although it could be profitable—to make an exhaustive study of this practice from the earliest Christian centuries. We wish here simply to be representative.

Before considering the Fathers, we might jump back even a step further and muse on Moses who descended the Mount of Sinai with his face radiant, following his encounter with Yahweh.[1] So awesome was his appearance that the Israelites would not approach him until he veiled his face, a practice he continued when among the people. He removed the veil whenever he entered the tent of Yahweh to give verbal expression to his prayer. The radiance was an outward sign of an inward grace. We are confronted here with a state or condition of soul, of intimacy with God that was not limited to moments and scheduled periods of formal prayer.

In the New Testament we are told by St. Luke that there was in Jerusalem a devout man, Simeon by name, who lived only to see the longed-for consolation of Israel.[2] Here was abiding prayer—desire, longing, yearning, expectation, trust—rooted as a disposition of the heart.

The prophetess Anna lived constantly in the temple, worshiping God day and night by her service, her fasting, and her prayer.[3] This bespeaks total commitment, a heart given over to God.

Mary, we learn, carefully meditated, ruminated, pondered all that happened to her, relating everything to God and solicitous about her relationship with Yahweh.[4] The content and tone of her canticle of praise show her to have been in intimate touch with God's saving action in Israel.[5]

The food of Christ's own life was his constant attention to his Father and his yearning to please him.[6] This longing and concern were so strong in him that he continually sought moments when he could be completely alone to commune in loving prayer with his Father. "He would always go off to some place where he could be alone and pray."[7] And there were times when "he spent the whole night in prayer to God."[8] This prayer was a being-with him whom he loved most ... his Abba, his Apa, his Papa.

The consuming fire of his heart broke forth in a blaze of radiant light and beauty on at least one occasion during his prayer—at his Transfiguring. Not his face only was aglow as with Moses, but his whole body. The *Shekinah*, the overshadowing presence of the Father was made manifest by the cloud as at Sinai and the Father responded to the Son's prayer with the filial acknowledgement, "This is my Son, the Beloved ..."[9] who would willingly be the New Covenant himself in his own blood.[10] The apostles trembled in astonishment and fear every bit as much as the Israelites before the first Moses descending from the mount of the Covenant.

St. John the Apostle found the satisfaction of his life, leaning on the breast of his Lord and learning the secrets of that Heart—which strengthened a love that saw him loyally at the foot of the cross with Mary.[11] Love/prayer at its deepest is a being-with and being-all-for the other.

In these few passing pre-patristic references, we see that something deep in the person, on the level of attitude, disposition, set of the heart, is the soul-pervading contact—yes, union—with God. So it was, even for the incarnate Son on earth. Such, then, is the deepest, richest meaning of unceasing prayer.

In the previous chapter we saw that the meaning coming to us out of the scriptural references to unceasing prayer rang the note of persistence or perseverence. In this chapter we are already seeing that this perseverence is carried along on a foundation of something rich and deep in the hearts of the persons presented thus far. As we move along we will see the unfolding of the relationship between these dispositions and unceasing prayer.

We turn now to some of the early Fathers.

St. Ignatius of Antioch. This inspired and attractive bishop of Antioch (died c.117) longed to see his journey to Rome end in the amphitheater; he feared lest influential Roman Christians would interfere with his being made a ground-wheat bread for Christ by the teeth of starved lions.[12] Was he thinking of the Eucharist and his share in Christ's sufferings and how he might feed Christ who has fed him as the pure Bread of Life? We see here a man whose whole preoccupation is Christ and how he might constantly serve him and express his love for him.

> Grant me no more than that you let my blood be spilled in sacrifice to God, while yet there is an altar ready ... I beg you, do not show me unseasonable kindness. Suffer me to be the food of wild beasts, which are the means of my making my way to God. God's wheat I am, and by the teeth of wild beasts I am to be ground that I may prove Christ's pure bread ... At last I am on the way to being a disciple. May nothing *seen* or *unseen*, fascinate me, so that I may happily make my way to Jesus Christ! Fire, cross, struggles with wild beasts, wrenching of bones, mangling of limbs, crunching of the whole body, cruel tortures inflicted by the devil—let them come upon me, provided only I make my way to Jesus Christ ... Permit me to be an imitator of my suffering God. If anyone holds Him in his heart, let him understand what I am aspiring to; and then let him sympathize with me, knowing in what distress I am.... My Love has been crucified, and I am not on fire with the love of earthly things. But there is in me a *Living Water*, which is eloquent and within me says: "Come to the Father."[13]

Ignatius, as a mystic, was acutely aware of the presence of God dwelling in the heart of the Christian; he tells the Ephesians that they are "God-bearers and temple-bearers, Christ-bearers and bearers of holiness."[14] Further on he exhorts them to "do all things in the conviction that he dwells in us. Thus we shall be his temples and he will be our God within us . . . Let us then love him as he deserves."[15]

Ignatius urges Polycarp, bishop of Smyrna and a future martyr as well, "To prayer give yourself unceasingly; beg for an increase in understanding; watch without letting your spirit flag."[16] We can't be certain here if Ignatius means anything more than to persevere in prayer to the end, given the context. But given the lives of these two men, they lived in constant prayer in that deeper sense of union and commuion with the Beloved.

Clement of Alexandria (died c.215). Clement, a serene and learned student of life, speaks of continual prayer in the final book of his Stromata (The Miscellanies) where he comments on how the committed Christian prays. He says specifically that prayer is converse with God, and that no opportunity of access to God by prayer ought to be neglected.[17]

What does he mean by converse? More than mere audible expression of petitions and needs, and more than scheduled periods of formal prayer. ". . . Not opening the lips we speak in silence, yet we cry inwardly."[18] He takes exception with those who are satisfied to pray only at some assigned time such as the third, sixth, and ninth hours; whereas, he teaches that we are to pray throughout our whole day and life. And he gives the reason: to endeavor by prayer to have "fellowship" with God, and to come to that perfection which is achieved by acting through the sweet power of love.[19] Thus converse is reaching toward intimacy expressive of what is deepest in the heart of the human person, far beyond articulation. "Being brought into close contact with the almighty power, and earnestly desiring to be spiritual, through boundless love, he is united to the Spirit."[20] Converse on this level is unceasing prayer.

In a passage that sounds rather like St. Paul, Clement says, "Holding festival in our whole life, persuaded that God is altogether on every side present, we cultivate our fields, praising; we sail the sea, hymning; in all the rest of our conversation we conduct ourselves according to rule."[21] And by rule he means the commandments and the practice of the virtues of a holy life. In a kindred passage he says,

> [The Christian's] whole life is a holy festival. His sacrifices are prayers, and praises, and readings in the Scriptures before meals, and psalms and hymns during meals and before bed, and prayers also again during night. By these he unites himself to the divine choir, from continual recollection, engaged in contemplation which has everlasting remembrance.[22]

Such prayer and love bears fruit that enriches others. Note in a final passage that he weds the Word, work and love:

> He impoverishes himself, in order that he may never overlook a brother who has been brought into affliction, through the perfection that is love, especially if he knows that he will bear want himself easier than his brother. He considers, accordingly, the other's pain his own grief; and if, by contributing from his own indigence in order to do good, he suffer any hardship, he does not fret at this, but augments his beneficence still more. For he possesses in its sincerity the faith which is exercised in reference to the affairs of life, and praises the gospel in practice and contemplation.[23]

Origen (died c.254). This mystic and son of a martyred father and himself tortured and crippled for his profession of Christ, wrote a treatise on Prayer which included a commentary on the Lord's Prayer. Origen says clearly what he sees to be the meaning of Jesus' and Paul's exhortation to pray without ceasing:

> He "prays without ceasing" who joins prayer to works that are of obligation, and good works to his prayer. For virtuous works, or the carrying out of what is enjoined, form part of prayer. It is only in this way that we can understand the injunction,"pray without ceasing," as something that we can carry out; that is to say, if we regard the whole life of the saint as one great continuous prayer. What is usually termed "prayer" is but a part of this prayer. . . .[24]

Like Clement, Origen sees a holy life of love, prayer and work as unceasing prayer. Life is a whole, and every "part" of it is meant to bring us or hold us in loving union with God.

St. Cyprian (died c.258) was a tower of strength by his faith and kindliness, ending his dedicated life as bishop of Carthage and "Pope" of Latin Africa by shedding his blood for Christ. He considers the frequency of prayer in the conclusion of his attractive little treatise entitled "The Lord's Prayer:"

> ... no hour is excepted for Christians, in which God should be adored frequently and always, so that we who are in Christ, that is, in the true Sun and in the true Day, should be insistent throughout the whole day in our petitions and should pray. . .[25]

It is apparent that Cyprian, more than the others we have reviewed, accepts ceaseless prayer in a rather radical way. Articulated prayer, and the intention and desire to adore and thank God frequently without an hour going by without some conscious expression of it is his ambition for himself and his people. But he goes even further:

> ... let there be no loss of prayers in the hours of the night, no slothful or neglectful waste of opportunities for prayer. Let us, who by the indulgence of God have been recreated spiritually and reborn, imitate what we are destined to be; let us who in the kingdom will have day alone without the intervention of night be just as alert at night as in the day; let us who are destined to pray always and to give thanks to God, not cease here also to pray and to give thanks.[26]

Thus, while Cyprian does not by any means neglect the works of piety and mercy as part of the Christian life—as is evident from his "Works and Almsgiving" and other treatises—yet he takes the exhortation to pray in a somewhat literal way. We will find this approach reaching a summit among the "monks of the desert," whom we will be examining below.

St. Basil the Great (died c.379). Descended from martyrs and saints, and raised in a family of saints, Basil the lawyer, monk and bishop, has greatly influenced Eastern asceticism and monasticism through his clear-sighted writings. He has also influenced Western monasticism, especially through the Rule of St. Benedict and all who have lived by it. In his *Regulae Fusius Tractatae* or *The Long Rules* Basil quotes the Scripture, "All things have their season."[27] He uses this text of Ecclesiastes 3:1 to point out that prayer and psalmody are not to be used as an excuse for neglecting work or any other obligation allotted its particular time. On the other hand, he adds that every hour is suitable for prayer and psalmody, so that,

> ... while our hands are busy at their tasks, we may praise God sometimes with the tongue (when this is possible . . .); or, if not, *with the heart*, at least, in psalms, hymns and spiritual canticles, . . . Thus, in the midst of our work can we fulfill the duty of prayer, . . . praying that the work of our hands may be directed toward its goal, the good pleasure of God.[28]

Following Basil further, we notice something interesting coming out of the expressions which I italicize:

> Thus we acquire a *recollected* spirit . . . *we keep before our minds* the aim of pleasing Him. If this is not the case, how can there be consistency in the words of the Apostle bidding us to "pray without ceasing" with those others, "we worked night and day." . . . each period contains a *reminder* peculiar to itself of blessings received from God . . . "I *remembered* God and was delighted."[29]

The italics in the texts quoted above—with the heart, recollected, keep before our minds, reminder, and remembered—point to an emphasis that is characteristic of St. Basil, who stressed *mnemē Theou (memoria Dei)*, i.e., mindfulness of God. As prayer, as unceasing prayer, the memory of God is much more than a simple remembering of the presence of God or an attempt to hold the thought of God in the intellect. Rather, it is an elan, an ardor, hinted at by the twist Basil gives to the Psalmist's line: "I remembered God and was delighted" ("groaned" in the original).[30] This elan inspires, moves, enables, the Christian to relate the many aspects of daily living to a loving God as a loving response. (We will have occasion to consider this again in the following chapter.)

In another passage St. Basil confirms his stance on continual prayer:

> We should not express our prayer merely in syllables, but the power of prayer should be expressed in the moral attitude of our soul and in the virtuous actions that extend throughout our life ... This is how you pray continually not by offering prayer in words, but by joining yourself to God through your whole way of life, so that your life becomes one continuous and uninterrupted prayer.[30a]

The Egyptian Desert Fathers. Almost simultaneously monasticism spread rapidly in a number of places, especially in Egypt, the Sinai desert, Palestine, Syria, Mesopotamia, Persia, Armenia, Asia Minor, and Gaul. We will consider here only the Egyptian monks, as representative of monasticism. More is known of these monks through extant primary source materials than of the other "deserts."[31]

Egyptian monasticism received its impetus from St. Antony the Great (died c.356 at the age of about 106) and from St. Pachomius (died c.346 at the age of about 56). St. Antony encouraged the hermitical life, both as anchorites living near one another in colonies or settlements, and as complete solitaries. St. Pachomius fostered the complete cenobitic life both for men and women by gathering them into large and carefully organized communities. These movements, of solitary and semi-community and full community life, gained momentum after the Peace of Constantine (Edict of Milan, 313 A.D.), which thereby opened the path for the churches to gain temporal power, honor, and possessions. It also opened the way for a flood of new and less-committed Christians who had less heart to oppose the values that shied away from the Cross. The moral fiber of the Christian populace gradually weakened. Hardier spirits looked for places free of worldly distraction from God and the pagan sensuality around them, seeking instead a life of asceticism and prayerful union with the Risen Lord and the hidden companionship of the martyrs. The martyrs matched life for Life and shed blood for blood. Now the "white" witnesses were replacing the red.

The monastic golden age glistened in Egypt during the

second half of the 300's. It was a time when it seemed like there were more monks inhabiting the deserts and wastelands than there were townspeople in the populated Nile valley.[31]a The flight to the ascetic combat of the desert crested near the year 400 when the Origenist controversy pitted the cultured Hellenized strain against the more primitive and basically biblically-minded Coptic monks. The former were banished from Egypt and drifted east in diaspora to the great benefit of the other "deserts," but to the decline and eventual decadence of Egypt. More of this history could be sought in its proper place, lest we get too far astray here, where we are interested only in framing the barest background for the monk's life of prayer.

Constantinian "freedom" and the ensuing politicizing of the Church stood in stark contrast with the ragged, simple, self-starved monks in their distant, sun-scorched "settlements." The trojan call of the times was to follow Jesus into the desert to struggle with fasting and the flesh, with Satan and the desire to have honor and power over fellow men. It was conversion. It was response to the "Sermon on the Mount." The life of the *anawim*, the poor of God. The life of the "Beatitudes": being poor in spirit, meek, in mourning, hungering, merciful, pure in heart, making peace, suffering whatever comes for the sake of the Lord. It was a wrestling with total dedication and commitment to Christ, with "no holds barred!"

The real saints of the desert were truly men of the Spirit, experienced in the ways of the desert combat, blessed with gifts that made them great lovers of the brethren, discerners of every spirit, and men of deep prayer. These "spiritual Fathers" ("Abbas" or Elders or Seniors, as they were called) coached the tyros who came into the desert, and these latter would eventually separate themselves from the Abbas to be on their own, or to live in two's or three's near the Abbas, or cluster in monastic colonies. The newcomers were "novices," becoming "the brethren" after some experience and separation. "Seasoned" brethren in their turn became Abbas.

Now it is precisely these desert monks, above all others who preceded them in Christendom, who as a body took the exhortation to "pray always" in its most literal sense. The personal struggle to succeed in this regard in the face of such barren circumstances is probably not widely appreciated. The following "apophthegm" or "saying" of the Fathers may give some hint of what went on in the heart of each desert saint:

> The brethren asked him [Agathon] "Amongst all good works, which is the virtue which requires the greatest effort?" He answered, "Forgive me, but I think there is no labor greater than that of prayer to God. For every time a man wants to pray, his enemies, the demons, want to prevent him, for they know that it is only by turning him from prayer that they can hinder his journey. Whatever good work a man undertakes, if he perseveres in it, he will attain rest. But prayer is warfare to the last breath."[32]

To digress for a moment, the apophthegms make much ado about demons. The danger for moderns is, then, not to take the sayings of the Fathers seriously. It helps to keep in mind that the Fathers assigned most of their unknowns of an antagonistic nature to demons which today we would see linked to the unconscious. In either case—whether attributed to an outside or inside source—the battle has still to be waged, with another or with self. If "another," there is a psychological advantage from the viewpoint of self-image, self-esteem and self-acceptance!

To "pray always" could also lead to the taking of sides with differing views, which on occasion erupted into open conflict. The heretical Messalians or Euchites (the word means pray-ers) were the "deep-enders," the extremists. Their stance is revealed in another apophthegm:

> Some of the monks who are called Euchites went to Enaton to see Abba Lucius. The old man asked them, "What is your manual work?" They said, "We do not touch manual work but as the Apostle says, we pray without ceasing." The old man asked them if they did not eat and they replied they did. So he said to them, "When you are eating who prays for you then?" Again he asked them if they did not sleep and they replied they did. And he said to them, "When you are asleep, who prays for you then?" They could not find any answer to give him. He said to them, "Forgive me but you

do not act as you speak. I will show you how, while doing my manual work, I pray without interruption. I sit down with God, soaking my reeds and plaiting my ropes, and I say, "God, have mercy on me; according to your great goodness and according to the multitude of your mercies, save me from my sins." So he asked them if this were not prayer and they replied it was. Then he said to them, "So when I have spent the whole day working and praying, making thirteen pieces of money more or less, I put two pieces of money outside the door and I pay for my food with the rest of the money. He who takes the two pieces of money prays for me when I am eating and when I am sleeping; so, by the grace of God, I fulfill the precept to pray without ceasing."[33]

Lucius says above that he spent his whole day working and praying; later we will see in what manner he accomplished this, and then too it will be more understandable why Agathon can say that prayer is a warfare!

That this struggle has its moments of contemplation and led to a holiness that was one heart with God and one heart with the brethren is manifest in the following apophthegms:

It is said of Abba Tithoes that when he stood up to pray, if he did not quickly lower his hands, his spirit was rapt to heaven. So if it happened that some brothers were praying with him, he hastened to lower his hands so that his spirit should not be rapt and he should not pray for too long [for the sake of not tiring or shaming the brothers with him].[34]

Doulas (who was at this time the disciple of Abba Bessarion), said: On another day, when I came to his (Bessarion's) cell I found him standing at prayer with his hands raised towards heaven. For fourteen days he remained thus. Then he called me and told me to follow him. We went into the desert. Being thirsty, I said to him, "Father, I am thirsty." Then, taking my sheepskin, the old man went about a stone's throw away and when he had prayed, he brought it back, full of water. Then we walked on and came to a cave where, on entering we found a brother seated, engaged in plaiting a rope. He did not raise his eyes to us, nor greet us, since he did not want to enter into conversation with us. So the old man said to me, "Let us go; no doubt the old man is not sure if he ought to speak with us." We continued our journey towards Lycopolis, till we reached Abba John's cell. After greeting him, we prayed, then the old man sat down to speak of the vision which he had had. Abba Bessarion said it had been made known to him that the temples would be overthrown. That is what happened: they were overthrown. On our return, we came again to the cave where we had seen the brother. The old man said to me, "Let us go in and see him; perhaps God has told him to speak to us." When we had entered, we found him dead. The old man said to me, "Come, brother, let us take the body; it is for this reason God has sent us here." When we took the body to bury it, we perceived that it was a woman. Filled with astonishment, the old man said, "See how the women triumph over Satan, while we still behave badly in the towns." Having given thanks to God, who protects those who love him, we went away.[35]

Deep union with God enables Abba Bessarion to taste some of the secrets of heaven, to experience power over nature, and to be sensitive to intuitions that accomplish works of mercy. The Abba is also seen here to be not only a spiritual father for his disciple, but a father in a fuller sense as one who fills up the needs of a son, even material. This is repeated in the following account ... which also gives us an insight into Bessarion's awareness of God and spontaneous trust in him:

Abba Doulas, the disciple of Abba Bessarion, said, 'One day when we were walking beside the sea I was thirsty and I said to Abba Bessarion, "Father, I am very thirsty." He said a prayer and said to me, "Drink some of the sea water." The water proved sweet when I drank some. I even poured some into a leather bottle for fear of being thirsty later on. Seeing this, the old man asked me why I was taking some. I said to him, "Forgive me, it is for fear of being thirsty later on." Then the old man said, "God is here, God is everywhere."[36]

It is very tempting to ask, "Who needs to sink a well with a friend like that around?"

Abba Arsenius succeeded in prayer the way he had succeeded at court as the cultured tutor of the emperor's son.

After abandoning his status and royal recompense, he fled secretly to Egypt and eventually found peace:

> ... on Saturday evenings, preparing for the glory of Sunday, he would turn his back on the sun and stretch out his hands in prayer towards the heavens, till once again the sun shone on his face. Then he would sit down.[37]

The disciple Lot—later Abba Lot—went to the Abba Joseph for some advice, and received the following "word":

> "Abba, as far as I can, I say my little office, I fast a little, I pray and meditate, I live in peace and as far as I can, I purify my thoughts. What else can I do?" Then the old man stood up and stretched his hands towards heaven. His fingers became like ten lamps of fire and he said to him, "If you will, you can become all flame."[38]

We can take it for granted that Abba Joseph did not reach such a state overnight. He lived for years going through a process of purification before God. Lot's self-disclosure to Abba Joseph gives us a summary of what these desert seekers were doing. All of the elements of their way of life were either prayer or oriented to prayer, and constituted incessant prayer.

Let's examine these elements as we get a picture of the Egyptian monk's day. His day began the night before. He usually arose from sleep around midnight and prayed his office of "Vigil" consisting of three "Nocturns" of four psalms each, frequently prayed in a standing position in his cell, alone, in the case of an anchorite. The cenobites prayed the Vigil together in an oratory or church, sitting, and listening attentively as a chanter sang or recited the twelve psalms. In either case, each psalm was followed by raising the hands in private *oratio* or prayer, then a brief prostration on the floor or ground, and a "collect" or summary prayer, standing, by the head of the cenobitic assembly. (The anchorite of course could adapt the pattern as he felt inspired, as exemplified above by Arsenius.) Also two passages of Sacred Scripture, one from the Old Testament and one from the New, were read and pondered.[39]

The Nocturns concluded, anchorites or cenobites spent

the remaining night hours in their cells praying until daylight, standing with outstretched arms and alternating with prostrations. Novices and brethren might use some of this time for reading and memorizing psalms and other Scriptures, and ruminating on their content. Breakfast was no problem—they never took food until noon at the earliest.

With daylight breaking into his cell the monk could continue his long day of prayer in another mode. When it was light enough for him to see, he would sit down to his work, something like weaving baskets or mats or braiding rope. As he worked routinely with his hands, his mind could become quiet, peaceful, reflective. He could call to mind a psalm verse and chew it over, let it lead him into affective prayer. Or he might choose to recite the psalms slowly and reflectively, saying the verses aloud, hearing the words, and letting his heart resonate with their meaning.

Stalwart monks fasted until the ninth hour of the day (approximately 3 P.M.), or until near sundown as in St. Antony's case. Vespers then completed the day with twelve psalms and twelve prayers. At dusk the monk lay down on his mat to sleep until the time for the night vigil and a new day.[40]

Of course this routine was occasionally or frequently modified to accommodate a journey for charity's sake, or for receiving a disciple or visiting monks. The Abbas maintained a certain fluidity and spontaneity along with their sensitive listening to the Holy Spirit (the Font of true spontaneity, directed toward God and neighbor).[41]

The monks of Egypt greatly favored the weaving skill for work because it helped the monk to sit quietly and to get rid of bodily restlessness and psychic agitation, while at the same time freeing him for unceasing prayer. The great Abbas of Egypt would hardly have agreed with St. Jerome, a monk himself in Bethlehem, in his letter to the young monk Rusticus of Toulouse in Gaul, when Jerome advised him not only to weave creels (wickerwork baskets) of reeds or pliant osiers but also to actively engage himself in far more engrossing forms of work:

> ... Hoe your ground; and when you have sown your cab-
> bage or set your plants, convey water to them in conduits;

... Graft unfruited stocks with buds and slips that you may shortly be rewarded for your toil by plucking sweet apples from them. Construct also hives for bees, for to these the proverbs of Solomon send you, and you may learn from the tiny creatures how to order a monastery and to discipline a kingdom. Twist lines too for catching fish, and copy books; that your hand may earn your food and your mind may be satisfied with reading. For "everyone that is idle is a prey to vain desires." In Egypt the monasteries make it a rule to receive none who are not willing to work; for they regard labor as necessary not only for the support of the body but also for the salvation of the soul. Do not let your mind stray into harmful thoughts . . .[42]

As is obvious, Jerome justifies his advice through the Scriptures to work in these various ways. Later Western cenobitic monasticism, especially the Benedictine, accepted this orientation toward agricultural development—and trades as well—just as Pachomian monks had done before them.

Jerome, however, by no means relinquishes the aim of incessant prayer for Rusticus, for he tells him:

... Never take your hand or your eye off your book; learn the psalms word for word, pray without ceasing, be always on the alert, and let no vain thoughts lay hold upon you. Direct both body and mind to the Lord, overcome wrath by patience, love the knowledge of Scripture, and you will no longer love the sins of the flesh. Do not let your mind become a prey to excitement . . .[43]

We can see here that fundamentally Jerome has the selfsame aims as the earlier monks, despite his own accentuations.

We can say that the monk's ultimate aim, as for every Christian, is union with God in the Life after this life. His immediate aim in this life is to pray always, even in conscious contemplative union, expressing perfect love of God and neighbor—in Cassian's language, perfect purity of heart. His particular manner of achieving his goal is precisely the monastic lifestyle, doing those monastic excercises which orient everything to God in an unceasing relationship of prayer.

In bringing this chapter to a close, we might note that the desert anchorites were able by their very life-style to accept the challenge to "pray always" in a more literal manner than the Christians who preceded them. This type of life has never been dominant in the West where the cenobitic form of monasticism has held overwhelming sway. In the East, as is commonly known, the anchorite life, both in full solitude and in the semi-solitude of the *laura* or *skete* has always been strongly evident and highly esteemed.

St. Benedict, following the orientation of Pachomius, Basil, and Cassian's Gallic cenobitism, attempted to put together a balanced community life of prayer offices, divine reading and physical work—the *Opus Dei, Lectio Divina* and *Opus Manuum.* His arrangement of these daily alternating elements in a pleasing-to-nature horarium and tempered ascesis established a life-style that was still ordered to the great Christian and monastic aim of praying always, yet modified enough to serve a broader spectrum of God-searchers. It "worked," as history gives evidence. Benedictine monasticism spread throughout the West and monasteries were filled with droves of men and women through the course of the Middle Ages, until they were accompanied and somewhat overshadowed by the rise of the later religious orders and congregations. These latter, instead of trying to build "far from the haunts of men" as the monks did and where they would eventually be surrounded by villages and towns anyway, went into the cities and on the highways, which of necessity occasioned more active expressions of incessant prayer: "contemplation in action," apostolates of mercy and missionary evangelization.

What Part Two (chapters three and four) is telling us is that in the Scriptures and the Fathers unceasing prayer indicates a number of different things, such as (1) frequently repeated, persevering prayer, which can gradually lead to (2) a continuing attitude, a disposition of soul, going far beyond something that is said from time to time and becoming something that one *is*. Out of this springs (3) the remembrance of God, *memoria Dei*, even as the works of love, daily tasks and duties, are accomplished. Not only are these levels of prayer not mutually exclusive, but they complement one another, support one another. Yet the second level remains the core.

And God is pleased to have sons and daughters who do not merely *say* prayers from time to time, but who *are* prayer all the time.

Part Three

Prayer Categories in the
Light of Unceasing Prayer

In the preceding chapter we witnessed a variety of ways in which praying without ceasing was taken by some of the early Fathers of the Church and the Desert Monks of Egypt.

Part Three will be an attempt to gather together a number of the usually suggested ways of touching God and, in categorizing them, to see them in the light of unceasing prayer. Despite the already numerous systems of classifying prayer, I will divide prayer into the following three groups: *Active, Dispositional,* and *Infused,* treating the first two together in Chapters Five and Six, and then treating Infused prayer in Chapter Seven.

Chapter Five

Active and Dispositional Prayer: A

I would like to call *Active prayer* and include under that title all of those ways of praying and acts of praying which we can accomplish because we ourselves deliberately choose and intend doing them, granting the assistance of God's grace.

Dispositional prayer would circumscribe our deep-seated, God-oriented habits, attitudes of mind, dispositions of heart, the whole underlying Spirit-responsiveness of our deep self. The outward signs, the voiced *ikons* of these depths are those unbidden, spontaneous expressions of the heart that know no distraction, nor special time nor place. The dispositions are known by their epiphanies; both are the fruit of spirit resonating with Spirit at the core of our being.

Infused prayer would pertain to those entirely gratuitous gifts of God whereby God "invades" the soul, the spirit, of man and inundates him with a sense of his presence or a sense of his absence, during which experience the human person is receptively passive rather than in any way active before God. The experience is frequently one of being loved with an overwhelming and indescribable love even while one's captured "gaze" is totally absorbed in the Divine Lover.

This classification of prayer in effect locates true constant prayer in the last two categories, namely, Dispositional and Infused. This should become clear by the end of this chapter. All other ways of praying are ways and techniques to nourish in us those dispositions that constitute this unceasing prayer, and to prepare the way for infused prayer if God wills us to receive it.

Now, we arrange *Active prayer* (prayer we choose and intend) into six convenient subdivisions:

1. Vocal prayer.
2. General intentional prayer.
3. Prayer of response to daily events.
4. Discursive prayer.
5. Affective prayer.
6. Prayer of simple "gaze."

1. Under *vocal prayer* we may include the *Pater* and the *Ave*, and combinations of these like the rosary, all prayer-book prayers, novenas, consecrations, stations of the Cross in set forms, litanies, the psalms and isolated verses, the hours of the Divine Office, and other little offices like that of the Blessed Virgin, hymns, pious aspirations, expressions of the Jesus Prayer, etc. These are prayers that may be "said" at set times or, if memorized, can be prayed also as one goes about routine works during the day. Besides "formulas" composed by others, we include here our own compositions.

2. Under *general intentional prayer* we can include the mental intention and desire to be united in some way with God, for example, to be "united with all of the Masses being celebrated throughout the world this day for the glory of God"; to "offer up" all of one's works, hardships, sufferings, joys and sorrows, and whatever is meritorious by being united with the life and sufferings of the Savior; to make a "pure intention" before beginning any good work or duty that it may be "done for God," i.e., done in harmony with his will or for his good pleasure; to intend to be "resigned" or "conformed" to God's will in all that we do and all that happens to us; etc. These "virtual" intentions have the note of offering our life to God and finding the offering acceptable to God by the power of these inner intentions of good will on our part, despite the possibility that we may be unmindful of God, his presence, and our offering, for most of the day's preoccupation with tasks and other persons, as can readily happen to anyone who has engrossing and heavy responsibilities.

3. In the *prayer of response to daily events* we would include those prayers which are occasioned in the person who is open to the divine possibilities in life's daily experiences, both exterior and interior. I would see this category differing from category two under the aspect of mindfulness of God and his presence, in the course of the day's activities. Here, then, we include our prayerful response to our crises, successes, joys and sorrows—in sickness, in bed or out, touching ourselves or our dear ones; our vocation, wedding or ordination or religious profession; temptations and inner struggles; in family, financial ups and downs, job or profession; graduations, travel and sight-seeing, banquets and other celebrations, pregnancies, interpersonal sharings, situations involving compassion and assistance, whether on the giving or the receiving end. It is open to everyone in everything.

A spectacular and heroic example of this prayer is at hand in the person of Mother Teresa of Calcutta. She has learned to take to heart the meaning and the consequences of the Gospel passage that assures us, ". . . insofar as you did this to one of the least of these brothers of mine, you did it to me."[1] She spends herslf hunting out the sick and dying, abandoned children, the helpless and miserable in every form—and this in the face of Calcutta's sweltering heat and humidity. She prays her work. The work itself deepens her union with Christ. Her work is the expression of her love for him . . . and that, through the way she goes about it. She does it for him, and she does it as *to* him.

Her heart murmurs expressions of love, spontaneous aspirations (which we will deal with later) and these are both "active" and "dispositional." But her dedication is such that it invites the God of love to infuse his treasures in her, making her all the more a vessel of compassion and service. Like her namesake of Avila, love received is love poured out. We see in her that doing the works of mercy with a generous and simple spirit has a way of expanding the heart with love and plunging us into the Heart of All Mercy. (Of course, these same works can also be an ego trip if we are self-centered rather than other-centered.)

In conclusion, event-prayer is the prayer of daily living—alert to seeing the divine where the divine is, in all of life . . . at work, at play, eating and resting, meeting with friends, in the silence of solitude, during the long nights of sickness, and the nine months of childing, through the fleeting years to full vision.

This possibility of finding God in everything and everyone is explained nicely in the following passage:

> ...The Christian experience of God seems to me to be characterized by its organic unity.... Whether one considers God from the point of view of the Trinity or the Creation or the Incarnation, he is *Gift*, and as such is immediately present to all reality. And reciprocally, any reality can mediate to us an authentic experience of this personal God. God is not primarily the Wholly-Other whom we can only encounter by leaving behind the human situation and entering either into the mystical void or into the sacred spaces of worship. He is the personal and loving Presence revealed fully in Jesus Christ and showing himself to every man in every situation, if only man is open to him. The immediate consequence is that in Christianity experience of God is infinitely broadened. For the really watchful person it could be constant, since every person and situation, in its inmost reality, is rooted in the Presence and Love of God. Moreover, what is required of us is equally broad. We are asked to be in a constant state of openness. We are not asked to leave some human space temporarily for a sacred space. We—that is, a few elect souls—are not asked to leave aside permanently the normal requirements of human existence for a desert of silence. We are asked, always and everywhere, through the Spirit of Jesus, to leave behind the first superficial level of any situation and find its second and lasting depth.

> ...There is a certain type of communication with others which, like the reading of Scripture, the contemplation of nature and the practice of certain techniques of recollection, is a direct revelation of God ... brothers seek to live and to communicate to each other a permanent experience of God, lived in openness to his grace.[2]

We return now to our remaining three categories of discursive, affective and simple "gaze" prayer. Many spiritual writers group these three together as forms of "mental prayer" and as such distinguish them from vocal prayer. I have chosen to group vocal as well as intentional and event-response prayer with mental prayer because I see them all as expressions of intermittent prayer, normally. And I have put them under the heading of "Active prayer" for the purpose of isolating them from those forms of prayer which I consider to be modes of unceasing prayer.

4. *Discursive prayer* is commonly called "meditation" and involves the industrious use of our imaginative and reasoning powers in addition to memory and volition, which are exercised on the mysteries of our faith and any and every aspect of our spiritual and moral life. There is no shortage of available literature on this way of praying, along with the several methods of procedure recommended by saints and holy writers (e.g., St. Ignatius of Loyola in his renowned *Spiritual Exercises*). I only mention it here to complete our schema.

5. *Affective prayer* is called such because feelings and expressions of affection predominate over the use of the imagination and reason. These warm affections frequently incite interior (i.e., silent) verbalization and sighing, and thus give rise to expressions such as "talking" or "conversing" with God in a loving manner. We normally slip out of discursive prayer and into affective prayer whenever we are moved with loving affection for God and temporarily cease to need intellectual and imaginative stimuli in relating to God. It is also a sign that faith, hope and love are becoming a ready and active part of our deeper self, causing us to turn spontaneously and joyously to God not only in set periods of "formal" prayer but also briefly during the course of daily activities and moments of rest. Whenever this prayer wells up in us we experience a pleasant readiness to do God's will, wishing to root out all of our faults and to live always in the loving presence of God. Consoling tears may frequently accompany this prayer, but also emotional fatigue. Since emotions oscillate, waver, ebb and flow, affective prayer alternates with frequent short periods of "dryness" (not the "infused dryness" of a later stage), which can periodically leave one feeling lonely, loveless and depressed—and feeling confused about one's prayer-life.

6. The *prayer of simple "gaze"* is a nearly wordless and

reposeful prayer. We slip into it when we get tired of "talking so much" to God, whom, we come to realize, knows all about us—much better than we know ourselves—and doesn't have to be told that we love him and want to die a martyr, or are ready to be a "victim-soul." (He knows our timbre and will slip us chips of the cross according to our growing strength.) So, our "monologue" is finished, and we are content simply to sit quietly "in his presence"—sometimes perceiving his presence, sometimes not.

There are many terms used to designate this level of prayer and each one seems to add a further note or nuance to the description of this prayer. Prayer of "simplicity" denotes the reduction of the ego activity of the mind, emotions and lips. Prayer of "simple regard," like simple gaze, indicates a beholding of the whole attractive reality in a single look rather than meditation's part by part and step by step inquiry and reflection ... more synthesizing than analyzing, much more of the intuitive than the discursive. "Active recollection" and "acquired contemplation" are pointing up the difference between passive (infused) recollection and infused contemplation. Active recollection is achieved by "calling in" all of one's human powers from their preoccupations and converging on God to be aware of his loving presence. Passive recollection achieves the same awareness, except that it comes about as a gratuitous gift of God, without the tension and toil of human effort, and with the gentle drawing of God inducing contentment of heart, unless the person disrupts it by his or her curiosity in trying to figure out what is happening. Acquired contemplation is telling us that it is possible to seek God and find him in simple faith and love by our sincere and practiced effort. Infused contemplation is all gift; and this expression covers many levels of divine visitation, from the barely perceptible to the diaphanous and ecstatic. "Prayer of the heart" is a term that one finds being applied by different writers to everything from affective prayer to the furthest reaches of infused contemplation, but as it is used here would indicate something of quiet affection and love for God, a total presence of the heart to God. "Centering" prayer has the note of moving through the surface levels of our conscious ego and functioning self to find God at the heart, the core, the center of our being, and staying "there" in his presence.

We must examine the six categories of *Active prayer* again; this time to notice the range of depth-level or degree of personal involvement operative in these modes of prayer. Before elaborating, we can say in brief that the range will vary from a mindless inattentiveness to a mindful attentiveness to a heart-full absorption. The last mentioned will bring us into the realm of *Dispositional prayer*.

Mindless inattentiveness. At its most miserable, vocal prayer can be rote recitation without attention or meaning, completely mindless, leaving the person questioning afterwards if the prayers were "said." An intentional prayer like a "morning offering" or an offering done out of habit before starting some duty or work can also be executed in an unthinking, unreflective way. Eventful experiences can often leave us with the haziest subconscious, ambiguous, contact with God. Since discursive, affective and simple regard prayer are usually given a scheduled period of time in our day, we may manage to spend the period—whether through fatigue, sleepiness, "out-of-sortsness" or whatever—in a dull, listless, mind-wandering, heart-not-in-it manner.

What beneficial effect does this hapless level of prayer have on our hearts, our inner depths? Not much, if any at all. Our convictions are not strengthened; no attitudes or dispositions are fashioned or fostered.

Mindful attentiveness. A more satisfying level is reached when we experience being mindful, attentive, in contact with our prayer. We are aware of what we are doing and are present to the meaning of the content. But this still does not necessarily mean that we are experiencing a personalized contact with God. If this contact is lacking, we do not experience a deepening of love, friendship and commitment. We are sometimes able to come away from the prayer with hardly more than a few "nice" thoughts, even "comforting" thoughts. There may be no penetration to the affective level, no touching of the whole person.

Heart-full absorption. And so, a far richer level of prayer is that in which we are not only attentive but moved in our inner depths. Inspirations bring us alive. We feel in touch with God and may become engrossed or absorbed in him. Not the bare meaning of words, but a personal relation with God is the heart of the experience. A sense of loving contact stimulates desire for God, a yearning for greater intimacy. We feel urged to repair our faults, to guard against moral failings, guard against anything that would displease God. We seek steps to give God a more central place in our life and to orient everything toward him; we rein in our ambitions and interests to harmonize with Christ's exhortations in the Gospel. Such expressions as ongoing conversion of heart, compunction, vigilance, resignation and conformity, prayerful spirit, presence of God, *memoria Dei*, as well as sensitivity to the welfare of others, spiritual associations, spiritual friendship ... such cease to be mere words mouthed by spiritual writers and speakers, but take on personal meaning and find a place in our life. They become an ever-deepening part of ourselves and gradually become deep-seated habits—patterns of thinking and acting as committed Christians. When they become a way of life for us, an orientation and commitment, we are living a life of constant prayer, a life of union with God. Putting prayer in these terms, we are dealing with three things simultaneously: the third level of prayer, *Dispositional prayer*, unceasing prayer.

As is evident, this level of prayer works deep changes in our personality and the relationship we experience with God. Disappearing are our erratic, whimsical, moody modes of conduct, which are gradually replaced by reasonable consistency and self-discipline, by inner-directed other-centeredness, in gentleness and compassion—all stemming from Christian attitudes of mind and loving dispositions of the heart.

We conclude also that all real, affective prayer (not speaking now of scheduled periods when we may or may not pray as a whole person) is on this third level of heart-full prayer. These fervent, spontaneous aspirations and cries of love in the silence of the heart are concrete expressions of this same dispositional and unceasing prayer. (Recall the prayer-example of Mother Teresa of Calcutta, above.)

Although these silent or audible expressions are intermittent prayer, they arise out of ever-deepening, stable dispositions of love and union with God which constitute dispositional prayer.

Let us bring this to a focus and a conclusion then by noting that the dispositional "shaping" of our being toward God is a silent habitual prayer, i.e., incessant prayer. And out of this dynamic condition of spirit arises a rich variety of fervent active prayer and forms of prayers, ranging from vocal to centering prayer, and opening the door even to God's gracious infusions of prayer.

Chapter Six

Active and Dispositional Prayer: B

Before considering *Infused prayer*, we will look once more at *Active* and *Dispositional prayer*. This time we will see several concrete forms of prayer as capable of being experienced at different levels.

By way of a first example take the family rosary situation. A member of the family group may be bored and inattentive, his mind elsewhere. It becomes a meaningless recitation and his mind is centered neither on the words nor the mysteries. Or, he can be basically attentive, reflecting on the words of the *Ave*, or inquiring into the mysteries, phantasizing their scenes, analyzing the import of what happened and how it applies to himself. We might think of this kind of participation as a "discursive rosary."

If he is drawn deeper, he may be touched and heartened by the *mirabilia Dei*, and his phantasizing and analyzing lessen and become secondary. ("Touched" and the like do not always have to be equated with joy, praise, contentment, etc., but also with alarm at our sinfulness, arousal to penance, fearfulness of infidelity or mediocrity, etc.) This would be an "affective rosary."

What about an "active contemplative rosary"? This would entail, not an unmindfulness, rather a mindfulness, but this time not on the mysteries and their implications. He would be subdued, peacefully mindful of God himself, absorbed in loving as the *Aves* slip by unattentively. Attention is "simply" on God who is fully meaningful during these alive moments.

The monk at his choral office and the diocesan priest at his private office could experience the same sort of bored inattentiveness, or searching attentiveness, or heartfelt involvement, or any combination of these. I wonder if it would be only at a choral office that one could be engaged on the level of intense active contemplation where the office is being carried along by others? It seems to me that if this level were reached in private recitation, the person would be continually losing his place, and have a difficult time completing the office. However, if one is enjoying the "simple presence of God" and is not much diverted or disengaged from what he is doing, this problem would not exist. Intensity would be the determining factor.

Digressing for a paragraph to make a clarification, there is another kind of inattentiveness which is neither boredom nor abstraction. It can happen during the office, the rosary, or during any period of prayer; we want to be very much present to God but the imagination is playing its TV and the mind is rambling over interesting events of the recent past or due to come up during the course of the day. Somewhere St. Teresa speaks of the imagination as being the "madman of the house" and elsewhere says that the mind "wanders about from place to place, like a fool finding no rest in anything."[1] And she continues, "The will however is attached to God so that this inner bustle causes much anguish..."[2] So, while we want to be prayerful and united with God we feel like a house divided against itself. And this is a condition that can only be borne with patiently. To add to such distress, this condition is often part of a larger and more painful purifying process, namely the passive nights of sense and spirit.

Litanies, and memorized aspirations said repeatedly, partake of the same vicissitudes and consolations and desolations as the foregoing. Now, however, spontaneous aspirations, for these spring from the deep self without distraction, as the melodies and plaints of the Holy Spirit. They are darts of love, and utterances of joy, praise and thanksgiving, and groans of pure sorrow and compassion. Again, these are expressions of dispositional prayer.

The Jesus Prayer—which is becoming better known and used in the West—begins with the lips as a memorized aspiration and verbalized expression and thus is subject to inattentiveness. This is normal of course. A certain amount of monotony and empty-headedness are part of the human condition. The Prayer is said to move from the lips to the head and then to the silent, wordless, thoughtless love of the heart to rest in an Abiding Presence.

The prayer of the gift of tongues, like the gift of any other form of active prayer which we are able to commence and terminate according to our own volition, is somewhat capable of distraction and a wandering mind.[3] On the other hand, it also lends itself to ardent prayer, especially when sung, and more especially yet, when it is sung in association with other Christians.

The "Our Father," which Jesus thoughtfully gave to us, has been a favorite vocal prayer-form used for discursive and affective prayer by Christians all down through the ages, and many meditative commentaries—ancient, medieval and modern—have been written on it. (Origen, Tertullian, Cyprian, Gregory of Nyssa, Augustine and John Cassian head the scroll; and 16th century Teresa of Avila[4] has written one of the most inspiring.) The "Our Father" is discursive prayer when we take it word by word and phrase by phrase, reflecting on each, savoring the meaning, and looking for applications or significance for one's own relationship with God. When the heart is attracted—which may happen frequently—spontaneous prayer wells up in affective "conversation," expressing all of the kindled yearnings of the heart. Prayer of simple gaze finds the divine Presence and the words cease. Or perhaps it is the haunting sense of loneliness for the Absent One that makes words difficult. One sits in silent desolation, looking for his presence, groping for what is not there. But it is this emptiness of heart that opens the way to receive the longed-for glimmer, and savors a loved one—a lover incomparably worth it all.

As a final example of a concrete form of prayer capable of being experienced at different levels, we turn to the monastic practice called *lectio divina*. At first thought, *lectio divina* may not seem to be prayer; this requires a word of explanation. The term *lectio divina* can be taken in two ways: as sacred reading alone, or more commonly as a peculiarly monastic "ladder of prayer,"[5] that is, as escalation of prayer or a process of prayer intensification. In the latter sense, *lectio divina* has four elements: *lectio, meditatio, oratio,* and *contemplatio.*

Here, we are interested, not in *lectio* as sacred reading alone, but in these four components. After a brief description of each one, we will see where they fit into our prayer categories.

Lectio divina is sacred reading both from the standpoint of the content and the aim or intention of the reader. That is, the content is specifically the divine revelation of God given to mankind; therefore, especially Sacred Scripture, and then other writings such as those of the Fathers of the Church who explained and homilized on the message of salvation; and sacred doctrine and theology. The aim or intention of the monk is prayer/communion with God. Therefore, the monk does not go to his *lectio* primarily for the sake of information but to stimulate prayer, to be inspired to remove from his life whatever is an obstacle to union, and to be moved to practice virtue. Understanding takes place and information is gathered, but this is secondary to the overall purpose of meeting God here and now. This sacred reading is prayer of desire to contact God.

Meditatio is not to be taken as discursive meditation (although that can be a part of it). Such would be a serious misunderstanding. *Meditatio* is not primarily reason working over and analyzing a passage, say of Scripture, but it is a work of memory, a faith imbued memory, applied to the message of salvation. Imagine the monk stopping short his *lectio* at a striking verse of Scripture: he sees it, says it, even says it aloud, hears it, tastes the sense of it through repetition, perhaps writes the verse in his note-pad or his journal; gradually the verse is fixed in his memory, may even touch his heart and enkindle his affections. When this happens, he is like a warm coal and tinder wood which breaks into flame—and this is *oratio. Oratio* is the fervent expression of love or joy or compunction or gratitude, etc.—in other words spontaneous aspiration, as we have seen it in this chapter. Cassian calls this "fire prayer" (*preces ignitas*).

And finally *contemplatio.* When the monk is drawn beyond

words and reduced to silence in the experience of God's presence, he has entered into contemplation. This may be "active"
or "passive," that is, "acquired" or "infused." In any case, *lectio*
has run its full course, aim has reached its blessed goal, intention its attainment. Reading stops, the book is forgotten, the
senses and memory repose, the fire ceases to leap and spark and
crackle—it has become silent glowing coals, the warmth of
love.

Equating this process to the categories of this chapter, we
can see that *lectio*, because of its aim, is like active prayer of
intention, desire, conformity; moreover, the very content, be it
Scripture, sacred doctrine, or whatever, carries it as prayer
even beyond intention and desire. *Meditatio* would readily
share the level of discursive prayer even though the two are not
quite the same, as indicated above. *Oratio* as mentioned already
is equated with spontaneous affective aspirations. And *contemplatio* stands for both acquired and infused contemplation.
As the former, it may be thought of as simple "gaze" or as
centering prayer. However, here, as part of the *lectio* process, it
is the culmination of the previous steps rather than a lengthy
scheduled period where one tries to quiet down and go quickly
into contemplation, which is what one tries to do, say, in a
period of centering prayer.

We have now finished with our concrete examples of
Active and *Dispositional* prayer and can move on to the third
category of prayer: *Infused.*

Chapter Seven

Infused Prayer

Much has been written on infused prayer (also called, infused contemplation, or mystical contemplation, or just mystical prayer). The mystics themselves have given us many inspiring accounts of their experiences as well as very sound teaching on this prayer. Here, I will limit myself to some comments that relate infused prayer to unceasing prayer.

First we must recognize that there is a difference between infused moments or "acts" of prayer and infused stages or states of prayer. We can certainly experience in early life isolated infusions which God gives for his own good purposes. Later in life when these moments become frequent or continuous, we say that we are in the "state" of that kind of prayer-experience. For example, it is not a rarity for young people, making a choice of vocation in life, to experience the isolated but reassuring assistance of what St. John of the Cross calls "substantial locutions";[1] likewise with the experience of "infused feelings," say, at the time of a retreat. However, when a Christian has arrived at that point where God in his goodness begins the process of personally cleansing his "earthenware vessel," we say that he or she is entering into the state of the night of the senses (the initial stage).

The "Night of Sense" is a period of purification where God in his loving mercy purifies us of imperfections which are so strongly wedded to our psyche that we cannot expose them and eradicate them by ourselves through self-discipline and the weapons of the spiritual warfare. It is a kenosis of sensual values in an over-sensed spirit which is not really free because dominated by attachments centering around sentiment, the romantic, the sexual, the "epicuric," around avarice, arrogance and vanity and the like. These disorders weaken and interfere with true God-centeredness.

The special grace received at this time stimulates a subconscious preoccupation with God which readily surfaces to awareness when we are not consciously occupied with duties and the engrossing activities of daily living. But the experience is not a consoling one normally because it surfaces in consciousness as a sense of God as absent, as gone, as distant, as can't-be-bothered-with-the-likes-of-me! Consequently the experience is open to serious misinterpretation by an unsuspecting soul who may read this ongoing experience as divine rejection . . . causing great distress of heart. And to some degree this is an unnecessary anguish. Fortunate is the person, in this case, who has available a good spiritual director who will lend encouragement and offset the possibility of despondency or even pathological depression. The director can lead the "directee" to get in touch with the inner person, the whole person. In due time the "directee" will discover that he or she does indeed have a sincere desire, a pervading desire for God. No small consolation! But better yet, he recognizes that "God has not really abandoned me; he is only trying to help me!" The sincere seeking of God is now recognized as having been cloaked in consciousness by the torment of apparently not "finding" him. The recurring floods of disordered affectivity, over-sensitivity and the ponderous temptations of narcissism can be suffered with greater equanimity. The frequent feeling of not "finding" God can be accepted as being an "OK-feeling" to have. The pressing feeling of loneliness will diminish. The desire for God will be recognized and appreciated as God's own gift. The purifying struggle can continue with gratitude in the realization that it will terminate in a truly intimate and unselfish love.

In this discussion of infused prayer, where do we locate unceasing prayer? It is precisely in the ongoing infused gift of desire for God. Even though this desire for God is often only subconscious or pre-conscious, it is "there," just as dispositions are always "there." The becoming aware of the desire and the manifest prayer that the desire gives rise to is kindred to the spontaneous aspirations and other overt expressions that stem from holy dispositions.

Insofar as desire for God is an orientation toward God it can also be considered a disposition. However, in this case, it is not a disposition acquired and deepened over time by one's sincere effort, but infused by God as sheer gift.

Having seen at this point that the initial state of infused prayer is at the same time unceasing prayer, we need not work our way through the succeeding stages of mystical prayer. They too are of necessity unceasing prayer. It would only remain to see what is the specific grace of each state, and then to perceive how it is unceasing prayer. This can be done easily by turning to some great mystic like John of the Cross or Teresa of Avila and read their masterpieces of mysticism. Unceasing prayer is evident at every step of the way.

As we near the end of Part III it might be of some value to point out three ways of approaching incessant prayer which are decidedly unenlightened. One way would be to interpret "pray always" in terms of verbalization and then attempt to maintain a continual stream of verbalized prayer during our waking hours. This was a severe strain even on the desert solitaries whose life style was arranged to enable them to keep up a constant flow of prayer, much of which did in fact find external expression. Even if this were attempted in the form of tongues, it would be imprudent. God does not expect it. Human nature is not built for it. And, most important of all, the effort may frustrate reaching a deeper, richer level of prayer. The worst example of this that I am aware of concerned a housewife who decided she must verbalize the rosary continuously throughout her workday. After a few days of headaches from her prodigious efforts and the resulting tension, she had the good sense to stop the ill-thought project. In a religious house this tendency may show itself in the choral offices by the effort to "say" the parts of both choirs; or, while the opposite side is reciting, to say some quick aspirations. Both are ill advised. It smacks of quantifying prayer, as if, "The more I say, the more God is pleased." Or even, "The harder I work at it and the more I exhaust myself, the more God is glorified." God is interested in our progress and desires to lead us from the exterior word to something deeper and less exhausting.

A second unenlightened approach to unceasing prayer would be to struggle to hold on to some image or concept of God during the whole day, or to fix the thought of some mystery of salvation in mind and to think about it from morning to night. It is an admirable endeavor, but the strain may produce a headache; the tenacity impede more fruitful forms of praying.

A third way is not uncommon for beginners in the practice of prayer. When the consolations, especially of affective prayer, begin to disappear, anguish or alarm may ensue, caused by a sense of insecurity. The presupposition here is that "I do not love God if I do not *feel* I love him." The consequence is a rash attempt to stir up fervor, to force a good feeling, and even to force "the loving tears of a repentant sinner." This won't help positive growth in prayer. Aridity and desolation will have to be faced, understood, lived through, and accepted as a necessary part of true spiritual purification.

However important unceasing prayer is, if it should by some misfortune be dissociated in anyone's mind from the love of God and his good pleasure, and the love of neighbor, it would be nothing less than catastrophic for his or her spiritual development. It would lead to further aberrations, for example, unhealthy withdrawal.

In summary, the burden of Part III has been to show that unceasing prayer is not achieved through active forms of prayer which are of necessity intermittent. Rather it is established through the far deeper level of dispositions of the heart, and through infused prayer bestowed by God. Active forms of prayer are certainly necessary, are themselves fruitful of union, intermittent union with God, and they foster the dispositions which are capable of being constant. Thus are we able to fulfill in a suitably human way the Gospel call to pray always. Furthermore, constant prayer via the development of such dispositions of heart is open, not only to monks, priests and religious dedicated formally to God, but to every Christian regardless of his or her vocation and situation in life.

Part Four
Three Techniques
for Fostering Unceasing Prayer

Part Four will be an attempt to describe three Christian "techniques"—using the term loosely—for fostering incessant prayer. All three have come down to us through the monastic tradition, both the Eastern and the Western.

In Chapter eight, we will treat of a method derived from the 14th century Cloud of Unknowing, which itself is rooted further back in the writings of the Pseudo-Dionysius (possible contemporary of St. Benedict, overlapping the 5th and 6th centuries). In its modern dress it is being given the name "Centering Prayer."

In Chapter nine, we will work on the Jesus Prayer, which has come to us through the rich treasury of the Eastern monastic tradition.

And in the final chapter we will consider the way of *lectio divina* which is such an intimate part of the Benedictine-Cistercian tradition.

Chapter Eight
Centering Prayer

Centering Prayer is based on the anonymous medieval writing called The Cloud of Unknowing, with some incidental helps from "Transcendental Meditation." After some extensive background material pertaining to The Cloud of Unknowing in order to see how the latter forms the basis for Centering Prayer, we will look at the modern setting and the steps of procedure for this prayer.

Background Material

For the person who has emerged from the purification of the Night of Sense there are moments of prayer, often long moments, when God holds him or her captive with awe and wonderment in his exquisite presence. Quite lost from self-awareness and completely taken up with so sweet a Father, the person is likely to spontaneously breathe in and out with a silent sighing love: "Fa ... ther!" ... "Fa ... ther!" over and over again, then fading into a silent fixity of attentive love and joy.

On other occasions this person may be moved to breathe a rhythmic: "My God!" ... "My God!" or "Je ... sus!" ... "Je-... sus!" When this moment of profound union with God has somehow slipped away, he or she may continue to pray quietly,

and perhaps wistfully longing for the Absent Lover. But if His
Presence continues in even an attenuated sense, one may continue consciously to savor those precious words: Father, Jesus,
Love, etc.—lingering over them as honey in the mouth. They
somehow help to embody or hold the affection, the gracious-
ness, the goodness of God; they in some way form an embrace
with the beloved. They stir love and invite love. They are
shafts of love.

I suspect that the anonymous author of The Cloud of the
Unknowing many times had such experiences, and he recognized how these precious words—richly laden with a divine
sweetness—breathed gently in the quiet of the heart had a way
of centering him in God and disposing him for further divine
encounters. If it should chance that his Lord remained hid, he
would continue his prayer of love in utter simplicity. It would
be prayer of a simple loving gaze.

This English author tells his young twenty-four year old
friend about this kind of prayer and the use of a word:

> A naked intent toward God, the desire for him alone, is
> enough.
> If you want to gather all your desire into one simple word
> that the mind can easily retain, choose a short word rather
> than a long one. A one-syllable word such as "God" or
> "love" is best. But choose one that is meaningful to you.[1]

He then goes on to explain why this word-technique helps
to sustain prayer:

> This word will be your defense in conflict and in peace.
> Use it to beat upon the cloud [not meaning: to strain] of
> darkness above you and to subdue all distractions, consign-
> ing them to the "cloud of forgetting" beneath you. Should
> some thought go on annoying you demanding to know
> what you are doing, answer with this one word alone. If
> your mind begins to intellectualize over the meaning and
> connotations of this little word, remind yourself that its
> value lies in its simplicity. Do this and I assure you these
> thoughts will vanish. Why? Because you have refused to
> develop them with arguing.[2]

This perceptive director, from his own experience, is able
to assure his "directee," "... If you strive to fix yourself on love
forgetting all else, which is the work of contemplation I have
urged you to begin, I am confident that God in his goodness
will bring you to a deep experience of himself."[3]

In a later chapter he is more explicit about the necessity of
discipline and the experience of God working in his heart:

> Don't you see how the Lord patiently supports you? Blush
> for shame! Bear the hardship of discipline for a short while
> and soon the difficulty and burden of it will abate. In the
> beginning you will feel tried and constrained but this is
> only because you do not yet experience the interior joy of
> this work. As time goes by, however, you will feel a joyful
> enthusiasm for it and then it will seem light and easy
> indeed. Then you will feel little or no constraint, for God
> will sometimes work in your spirit all by himself. Yet not
> always nor for very long but as it seems best to him. When
> he does you will rejoice, and be happy to let him do as he
> wishes.[4]

Continuing, he indicates something of the nature of God's
visit in terms of light and the affection of love:

> Then perhaps he may touch you with a ray of his divine
> light which will pierce the "cloud of unknowing" between
> you and him. He will let you glimpse something of the
> ineffable secrets of his divine wisdom and your affection
> will seem on fire with his love. I am at a loss to say more,
> for the experience is beyond words.[5]

While pointing out that distractions are the bane of this
prayer as with every other lesser form, he is confident of a
quick recovery: "... No sooner has a man turned toward God
in love when through human frailty he finds himself distracted
by the remembrance of some created thing or some daily care.
But no matter. No harm is done; for such a person quickly
returns to deep recollection."[6]

He goes on to caution against striving to develop this
prayer by using the mind and imagination: "... Be careful in

this work and never strain your mind or imagination, for truly you will not succeed this way. Leave these faculties at peace."[7] And he gives a reason: "... The intellect of both men and angels is too small to comprehend God as he is in himself."[8] Rather this is a work of love alone:

> No one can fully comprehend the uncreated God with his knowledge; but each one, in a different way, can grasp him fully through love. Truly this is the unending miracle of love: that one loving person, through his love, can embrace God, whose being fills and transcends the entire creation. And this marvellous work of love goes on forever, for he whom we love is eternal. Whoever has the grace to appreciate the truth of what I am saying, let him take my words to heart, for to experience this love is the joy of eternal life while to lose it is eternal torment.[9]

He adds another note to the reward of this love and this prayer in the succeeding paragraph:

> He who with the help of God's grace becomes aware of the will's constant movements and learns to direct them toward God will never fail to taste something of heaven's joy even in this life and, certainly in the next, he will savor it fully. (And immediately the motivating question:) Now do you see why I rouse you to this spiritual work?[10]

It is surely evident that he is urging prayer of simple loving gaze, not discursive meditation or affective "conversation." "I tell you that everything you dwell upon during this work becomes an obstacle to union with God. For if your mind is cluttered with these concerns there is no room for him."[11]

But perhaps it is not clear yet to what extreme he carries his caution against thinking and imagining, and how strongly he advocates letting the mind rest in simple loving awareness of God in himself:

> Yes, and with all due reverence, I go so far as to say that it is equally useless to think you can nourish your contemplative work by considering God's attributes, his kindness or

his dignity; or by thinking about our Lady, the angels, or the saints; or about the joys of heaven wonderful as these will be. I believe that this kind of activity is no longer of any use to you. Of course, it is laudable to reflect upon God's kindness and to love and praise him for it; yet it is far better to let your mind rest in the awareness of him in his naked existence and to love and praise him for what he is in himself.[12]

It is time to recognize that this is not a form of prayer for stark beginners. The author of these instructions is clear on this point: "... Anyone who expects to advance without having meditated often on his own sinfulness, the Passion of Christ, and the kindness, goodness, and dignity of God, will most certainly go astray and fail in his purpose."[13]

But who then is ready for this prayer and what does it demand of him? "... A person who has long pondered these things must eventually leave them behind beneath a 'cloud of forgetting' if he hopes to pierce the 'cloud of unknowing' that lies between him and his God."[14]

And for what is the sign to look? When should one begin?

Whenever you feel drawn by grace to the contemplative work and are determined to do it, simply raise your heart to God with a gentle stirring of love. Think only of God, the God who created you, redeemed you, and guided you to this work. Allow no other ideas about God to enter your mind. Yet even this is too much. A naked intent toward God, the desire for him alone, is enough.[15]

In the final chapter of this marvelous little book the author offers three test signs for discerning when God is calling a person to move on to this kind of prayer:

In the first place, let a man examine himself to see if he has done all in his power to purify his conscience of deliberate sin ... let him see if he is habitually more attracted to this simple contemplative prayer than to any other spiritual devotion ... And then, if his conscience leaves him no peace ... unless he makes this ... his principal concern, ...[16]

In another little book by the same author, called The Book of Privy Counseling, he takes up the same topic of discernment and has this to say:

> But most of all, he must learn to be sensitive to the Spirit guiding him secretly in the depths of his heart and wait until the Spirit himself stirs and beckons him within. This secret invitation from God's Spirit is the most immediate and certain sign that God is calling and drawing a person to a higher life of grace in contemplation.[17]

And how are we to recognize this invitation of the Holy Spirit? By a "gently mounting desire to be more intimately united to God."[18]

The Modern Setting

With The Cloud as background, let us now look at the modern setting of this kind of contemplative prayer. Upon the encouragement and active support of Abbot Thomas Keating, a monk of St. Joseph Abbey, Spencer, Massachusetts, Father William Meninger, devised a technique for introducing interested guests and visitors of the monastery to the prayer set forth in The Cloud of Unknowing. Another monk of the same abbey, Father Basil Pennington, helped to develop a workshop in which to communicate this method of "Centering Prayer" for the Religious Life Committee of the Conference of Major Superiors of Men in 1975. During his work Father Basil popularized the name "Centering Prayer." Meanwhile, Father William and Father Basil have continued to offer a workshop at the abbey not only to initiate the participants into Centering Prayer, but to train them to become teachers of the method. There are now a number of centers around the country where the method is being taught, and new centers are continually springing up.

Dom Thomas Keating, explaining Centering Prayer at a meeting of Cistercian novice directors in January of 1976, said that the name "Centering Prayer" was inspired by the late Thomas Merton's emphasis on passing beneath the level of one's surface self, the empirical self, and entering into one's "heart" and finding God in the core, the center of one's own being. "The Kingdom of God is within you."

Centering Prayer has certain similarities with Transcendental Meditation due to the adoption of some secondary elements from T.M. There are also some profound differences.

Centering Prayer is Christian prayer; therefore, like that of the author of The Cloud, it is grounded in a faith stance in Divine Revelation. On the other hand Transcendental Meditation .claims to be non-religious. Centering Prayer fosters a personal relationship; Transcendental Meditation is non-personal. Centering Prayer is a call of God to Divine Friendship, to a union in love; Transcendental Meditation is a way for some adherents to enter into the "absolute," but for most it is a way to achieve more mundane aims, both bodily and psychic— to feel better, to become less dependent on liquor, cigarettes, drugs, to lessen tension, reduce high blood pressure, to be able to think more clearly, to gain self-control, improve efficiency, to need less sleep, to use as a non-chemical tranquilizer, to find peace of mind, etc. If Centering Prayer attains these same mundane benefits, they are considered merely secondary advantages.

The similarities of Centering Prayer and Transcendental Meditation are several. Both techniques recommend a sitting position, relaxing with eyes closed, for a period of twenty minutes, twice a day, with the help of a word or mantra to reach interior silence. At first sight it looks as if all of the mechanics of Centering Prayer have been borrowed from Transcendental Meditation. On closer examination however it is clear that the author of The Cloud mentions some of these. He says, "Simply sit relaxed . . ." (chap. 44). For him and for Centering Prayer the word must not be a meaningless sound as in Transcendental Meditation but as he says, ". . . Choose one that is meaningful to you" (chap. 7). Although he does not mention it, it is not unthinkable that he closed his eyes to assist his "naked intent toward God" since it is quite a natural thing to shut one's eyes to close off visible distractions. As a solitary, the author of The Cloud hardly limited himself to two brief twenty-minute periods of prayer each day; Father Basil suggests periods of twenty minutes as a starting minimum, while remaining open to expanding the time as the inclination is felt. And he considers two such periods per day as minimal, not as the norm as in T.M. (In fact he urges the ongoing practice of the prayer in places of waiting, such as the airport and on public transportation.) Father William suggests much the same, realizing that each individual must experience for himself or herself how often and how long would be personally beneficial.

A contribution of Transcendental Meditation was simply to put these monks on the track of working up a technique in more explicit terms than is readily recognizable in a first reading of The Cloud. Dom Thomas explains that the chief borrowing from T.M. is in the packaging of the workshop, that is, "we were inspired by our experience of initiation into T.M. to try to put the teaching of The Cloud and of Christian tradition into a similar concentrated form that could be easily communicated. This consists of an introductory lecture or two, conceptual background given in the course of the workshop, but most of all actually meditating together and answering practical questions about difficulties that may arise. . . . A few expressions and phrases both on Father William's tapes and in Father Basil's forthcoming book, Daily We Touch Him (Doubleday), are borrowed from T.M. instructors, but these are incidental."[18a]

These monks have received a very favorable response both from lay visitors to the monastery and from many religions. The recent and ever-increasing interest in mysticism outside of Christianity is obviously having a repercussion within Catholicism, as many religious discover in their own hearts the secret yearning for the contemplation urged by the author of The Cloud and The Book of Privy Counseling.

Practical Procedure for Centering Prayer

The heart of the "method" is summed up in "Three Rules." I will give Fr. William Meninger's version which I culled from his cassette recordings.[19] I will also give Fr. Basil Pennington's (from his article in Review for Religious[20]) in alternation with Fr. William's, and in italics.

Rule One: Begin your meditation with a half minute act of faith and conclude it with a two-minute "Our Father" or another prayer. *At the beginning of the prayer we take a minute or two to quiet down and then move in faith to God dwelling in our depths; and at the end of the prayer we take several minutes to come out, mentally praying the "Our Father."*

Rule Two: Choose a prayer that you deliberately will to make as an expression of your love of God and gently concentrate on listening to it. *After resting for a bit in the center in faithfull love, we take up a single simple word that expresses this response and begin to let it repeat itself within.*

Rule Three: When you become aware that you have stopped your prayer, you say to yourself, "I will go back to my prayer." *Whenever in the course of the prayer we become aware of anything else, we simply gently return to the prayer word.*

These two expressions of the Rules are essentially the same, and this is confirmed by comparing the accompanying explanations of the cassettes and printed article, which we cannot go into here.

Using material from the cassettes and the article, as well as my notes from Dom Thomas Keating's sharings at the meeting of Cistercian novice directors at Holy Spirit Abbey in 1976, I will attempt now to lay out "organically" the step-wise procedure for practicing this form of prayer.

First, select *a room or a place* where we know we will not be disturbed. Absence of noise is not necessary, but absence of intrusion is.

Next, *take up a sitting position that is relaxing*, but with good posture, on a chair—the new breed might prefer a cushion, a rug, or the floor with back against the wall.

Now we *begin with some expression of faith*, formal or spontaneous, to relate ourself in faith-surrender to God dwelling in the core of our being. This prayer is limited to a half minute purposely to prevent slipping away into a discursive meditation.

Establish deep regular breathing, and then, if helpful, a bodily relaxation exercise should follow. Moving from the feet to the scalp, each muscle in turn is quietly ordered to relax, consciously imaging the muscles at ease.

(Fr. William proposes the faith-prayer before deep regular breathing and bodily relaxation; Fr. Basil reverses the order.)

Now, (quoting from The Cloud), *"Center all your attention and desire on him* [God] and let this be the sole concern of your mind and heart" (chap. 3). This centering in faith/trust/love is the whole essence of the prayer.

Maintain this loving attentiveness and surrender by using a word. (Fr. Basil: "a single simple word;" Fr. William: "a prayer of no more than four syllables" e.g., Abba-Father.) The longer the expression the greater the danger of intellectualizing and fall-ing into discursive prayer. The vocative case is best because it is personal, relating us to someone in whose loving presence we are—Father! God! Jesus! Lord! Love! Let the word "take its own pace, louder or softer, faster or slower; it may even drift off into silence. 'It is best when this word is wholly interior without a definite thought or actual sound' (The Cloud of Unknowing, chap. 4)."[21] The ideal, then, is to speak the word mentally "without moving lips, tongue or vocal cords;"[22] the word may become completely interiorized until only the heart is praying it. Moreover, "the quiet mental repetition of the word-prayer" should not become "an effortful repetition of an ejaculation."[23]

During the ensuing minutes of the prayer period, *our stream of consciousness will frequently surface images and thoughts of daily cares and life's involvements.* These will be attractive like colorful boats or repugnant like ugly debris floating down the stream. "No harm done," says The Cloud (chap. 4). When we become aware of them, we do not attack them vigorously, and thus get excited, but *"gently return to the prayer-word."* In this case the word becomes "a vehicle to go from the boats and debris to the stream at its Source."[24]

On the other hand, images and thoughts that are related to desires and fears have a way of tensing us, shortening our breathing and tightening our muscles. When we become aware of them and give way to voluntarily thinking about them, we depart from praying and lose the restful presence of God. If, instead, we quietly return to the prayer-word, "the thought or image with its attendant tension will be released and flow out of our awareness."[25]

When the prayer period is nearly over, the prayer-word is discon-

tinued. The silence, our sense of restful receptivity, the Divine Presence will, one or all, fill our consciousness. And we will be at peace. We will be aware (post factum) of having quieted down and reached a deeper level of consciousness. (Sometimes more deeply than others.) *After a few moments we conclude the prayer by mentally or interiorly beginning the "Our Father."* We take it very slowly, tasting it phrase by phrase. "We savor them, enter into them. What matter if in fact it takes a good while. It is a beginning of letting our contemplative prayer flow out into the rest of our lives."[26]

Some Explanatory Comments

We might ask if it is appropriate to speak of technique or method—an orderly process to achieve an end or goal— when we are dealing with prayer at the depth-level of contemplation. We might be able to methodize ourselves, but we certainly will not methodize God who is totally free. And this is what Fr. William proposes, that our method is for ourselves, to help us to be open, to be exposed and receptive to contemplative prayer, to this gift of God. He says, "We don't have to worry about God's part; what we should be concerned about is what *we* should do."[27]

But once we have begun praying in this way, what about other forms of prayer? Fr. William advises prudence; there will be times when we will need and will feel moved to pray discursively and affectively, and we should do so. Follow the lead of the Spirit.

Nevertheless, it is good to see how pure this contemplative prayer is. In the words of Father Basil: "In active forms of prayer we use thoughts and images as sacramentals and means for reaching out to God. In this prayer we go beyond them, we leave them behind, as we go to God himself abiding in our depths. It is a very pure act of faith."[28] And he continues strikingly, "Perhaps in this prayer we will for the first time really act in *pure* faith. So often our faith is leaning on the concepts and images of faith. Here we go beyond them to the object himself of faith, leaving all the concepts and images behind."[29]

In line with this faith we might notice also that during the course of a prayer period when we become aware that we have stopped praying and are occupied with thoughts about a care or a fear, if we deliberately cut off the thinking and return to prayer, we are doing a significant thing. The very gesture of returning to prayer is a manifestation of faith and love. It is a dying with Christ in faith, for Christ—and this is love. Then in silence, in listening, we rise to the new life that is given to us through what God does for us.

More specifically, this rising to a richer life becomes even a temporal reality at those moments when we lose sight of the prayer-word and all awareness of ourselves, not now through any distraction, but through an absorption, a being "oned" with God. And there we become "oned" with all of his creation. It is by happenings like this that we "take possession of our real transcendent relationship with God in Christ," and also "our real relationship with each and every person in Christ."[30]

In keeping with the silent, receptive, surrendering nature of this prayer in which we meet God with utter openness and on his terms, so to speak, a word that expresses a response of waiting on God at the "meeting-place" with the utter openness of faith and receptive love, is just "being," being for God, so that he can give himself as he sees appropriate. This, in my view, is *anima*, a stance of femininity, which is the only possible stance if the Divine Lover is to be free to infuse his mystic graces. The element of femininity is thus a factor in the mystical experience.

Finally, both Fr. William and Fr. Basil indicate the effects of this way of praying. Prayer of such a deep level is bound to have a marvelous influence on other areas of our lives. Especially will we experience the maturing of the fruits of the Holy Spirit: love, joy, peace, patience, benignity, kindness, gentleness—deification of the *anima*. And we will find an increasing ability, "connaturally, as it were, to experience the presence of God in all things, the presence of Christ in each person we meet. Moreover, we sense a oneness with them. From this flows a true compassion—a 'feeling-with.' "[31] Our hearts will be so shaped that we are in reality a living prayer, the embodiment of incessant prayer.

Chapter Nine

The Jesus Prayer

The Jesus Prayer, and devotion to the Holy Name in general, touches the living center of Christianity. "For of all the names in the world given to men, this is the only one by which we can be saved."[1] Jesus means "savior." And Jesus *is* the Savior.

Background

Devotion in the West has found expression in many beautiful invocations and hymns in honor of the Holy Name. One of the most attractive poetic expressions to come down to us in the hymn "Jesu, dulcis memoria"[2] which bears relating here as it contains the sentiments and affection hidden in the Jesus Prayer.

Jesus, the very thought of Thee
With sweetness fills the breast!
Yet sweeter far Thy face to see
And in They presence rest.

No voice can sing, nor heart can frame,
Nor can the memory find,
A sweeter sound than Jesus' name,
The Savior of mankind.

O hope of every contrite heart!
O joy of all the meek!
To those who fall, how kind Thou art!
How good to those who seek!

But what to those who find? Ah! this
Nor tongue nor pen can show—
The love of Jesus, what it is,
None but His lovers know.

Jesus! our only hope be Thou,
As Thou our prize shalt be;
In Thee be all our glory now,
And through eternity. Amen.

In the East, the Jesus Prayer was the point of convergence of this piety toward the Holy Name. It has a long ancestry. We find it even in the Gospels when the ten lepers cried out from a distance, "Jesus! Master! take pity on us."[3] And the blind beggar, Bartimaeus, sitting by the road and hearing that Jesus was passing by, shouted out, "Son of David, Jesus, have pity on me."[4] Another Gospel account of the two blind men outside Jericho calling out persistently, "Lord! Have pity on us, Son of David."[5]

We must grant that Jesus was approached with a different kind of faith and reverence in his pre-resurrection days. He was taken for a healer, a prophet, a descendent of David—minus throne, palace, kingdom, and royal harem. He was taken as a "son of God," but hardly as *the* Son of God. Yet this faith sufficed for him to be able to do his work of healing and to prepare hearts for his revelation of the Father, himself and the Holy Spirit.

"Jesus is Lord" and "Come, Lord, Jesus!" were post-resurrection cries of divine faith and longing expectation. The Liturgy heard the repeated appeals, "*Kyrie, eleison,*" "*Christe, eleison.*" "Through him," exhorts the author of the Letter to the Hebrews, "let us offer God an unending sacrifice of praise, a verbal sacrifice that is offered every time we acknowledge his name."[6]

From then onward, we find devotional invocations to Jesus in a variety of forms, using his various titles of Lord,

Christ, Son of God, Everlasting King, Son of the Father, etc.

We find the prayer flowering in the desert among the monastic Fathers:

> Abba Macarius was asked, "How should one pray?" The old man said, "There is no need at all to make long discourses; it is enough to stretch out one's hands and say, 'Lord, as you will, and as you know, have mercy'. And if the conflict grows fiercer say, 'Lord, help!' He knows very well what we need and he shows us his mercy."[7]

The Abba Isaac, one of the teachers of John Cassian, adopted and adapted the leading verse of Psalm 69 as his appeal to Christ: "O God, make haste to my rescue; Lord, come to my aid." The Abba shared a colorful description of his use of this prayer in his colloquy with John Cassian.

> I am affected by the passion of gluttony. I ask for food of which the desert knows nothing, and in the squalid desert there are wafted to me odors of royal dainties, and I find that even against my will I am drawn to long for them. I must at once say: "O God, make haste to my rescue; Lord, come to my aid."

> Weakness hinders me when wanting severer fasts, on account of the assaults of the flesh, or dryness of the belly and constipation frightens me. That the fire of carnal lust may be quenched without the remedy of a stricter fast, I must pray: "O God, ..."

> When I want to apply myself to reading, a headache interferes and stops me, and at the third hour sleep glues my head to the sacred page, an overpowering desire to sleep forces me to cut short the rule for the Psalms: in the same way I must cry out: "O God, ..."

> I am tried by being puffed up by accidie, vainglory, and pride, and my mind with subtle thoughts flatters itself somewhat on account of the coldness and carelessness of others: In order that this dangerous suggestion of the enemy may not get the mastery over me, I must pray with all contrition of heart: "O God, ..."

Perhaps wandering thoughts career about the soul like boiling water, and I cannot contest them, nor can I offer prayer without silly mental images interrupting it; I feel so dry that I seem incapable of spiritual feeling, and many sighs and groans cannot save me from dreariness: I must say: "O God, . . ."

Again, I feel that by the visitation of the Holy Spirit I have gained purpose of soul, steadfastness of thought, keenness of heart, with an ineffable joy and transport of mind, and in the exuberance of spiritual feelings I have perceived by a sudden illumination from the Lord an abounding revelation of most holy ideas which were formerly altogether hidden from me: in order that it may linger for a longer time I must often and anxiously exclaim: "O God, . . ."

Encompassed by nightly horrors of devils I am agitated and am disturbed by the appearances of unclean spirits, my very hope of life and salvation withdrawn by the horror of fear. Flying to the safe refuge of this verse, I will cry out with all my might: "Oh God, . . ."

Then the Lord restores and consoles me, and suddenly I can dare to go out to face the enemy and provoke them to fight when a moment before I was trembling with fear of death and shuddering in mind and body at their touch or proximity. To abide by God's grace in this strength and courage, I must say with my whole heart: "O God, . . ."

We must then *ceaselessly* and *continuously* pour forth the prayer of this verse, in adversity that we may be delivered, in prosperity that we may be preserved and not puffed up. Let the thought of this verse, I tell you, be conned over in your breast *without ceasing*. Whatever work you are doing, or office you are holding, or journey you are going, *do not cease* to chant this When you are going to bed, or eating, and in the last necessities of nature, think on this. *This thought in your heart may be to you a saving formula*, and not only keep you unharmed by all attacks of devils, but also purify you from all faults and earthly stains, and lead you to that invisible and celestial contemplation, and carry you on to that ineffable glow of prayer, of which so few have any experience.[8]

We may note once more from the final paragraph of the above passage the ideal of unceasing prayer. The early monastic fathers struck upon an assortment of short prayers, scriptural invocations, repeated in the heart, with great frequency, as an aid in satisfying their ideal. Invocations which incorporated the Holy Name of Jesus gradually won preference.

The Jesus Prayer appears also in the One Hundred Chapters on Spiritual Perfection by Diadochus, Greek bishop of Photike in Epirus (died in the second half of the Fifth Century). In his chapter on the "Remembrance of God: Invocation of the Name of Jesus," Diadochus sounds remarkably like the anonymous author of the Cloud of Unknowing, recommending a word-prayer to quiet the mind and imagination and to open oneself up to the experience of God. This fifth century contemplative says that when we turn ourselves over completely to centering on the remembrance of God, we must satisfy the intellect's restlessness and need for activity via an invocation, and he suggests "Lord Jesus." This prayer is to be its only occupation. And he goes on to claim that anyone who "holds this holy and glorious Name unceasingly in the depths of his heart will come to enlightenment." By an intense experience, all stain will be wiped away because "Our Lord is a consuming fire." "The Lord attracts the soul to a great love of his own glory." With affection of heart the invocation of the Name "implants in us the disposition of unrestrained love of God's goodness;" and brings us the strength of humility and holy tears without sorrow. And thus we arrive at an ineffable joy.[9]

There is a very beautiful text found in the Philokalia that was attributed to St. John Chrysostom:

> A monk . . . must continually cry: "Lord, Jesus Christ, Son of God, have mercy upon me!" . . . He should always live with the name of the Lord Jesus, so the heart absorbs the Lord and the Lord the heart, and the two become one.[10]

Although providing us with the full formula of the Jesus Prayer, and recommending it as a means to achieve the deepest form of incessant prayer through becoming one heart with Christ, this particular passage is now recognized as not belonging to Chrysostom and must be dated several centuries later.

Father Kallistos Ware says, "There is no explicit and definite evidence for the prayer, in its fully developed form, before the sixth century."[11] And when exactly the prayer became linked to a technique of breathing is likewise uncertain. St. John Climacus (died c.649) and other earlier Eastern Fathers speak of breathing in conjunction with the invocation, but it is not clear if they mean a true synchronizing of breathing with the prayer. However, by the time of the great hesychastic revival among the monks of Mt. Athos in the 1200's and 1300's both the full form of the invocation and the breathing exercise are in abundant evidence.

Now, without drawing out the historical development any further, let us consider what the Jesus Prayer is. From what we have seen so far, we can at this point realize that it is:

an invocation (a calling upon someone, a plea, a prayer)
directed to Jesus, the risen Lord
as a real, living, Person
our only Savior
involving a relationship of faith and love
(or at least a desire to believe and love)
which leads us, according to his promise and gift,
to a sense of his loving presence
and a personal communing with him.
(Recall the striking Johannine texts which we considered
   in Chapter 2 concerning Jesus' promise and gift of himself.)

The Formula of The Jesus Prayer

The common formula that developed among the Byzantine monks was the seven word expression: *Kyrie Iesou Christe, Huie Theou, eleison me.* That is, "Lord Jesus Christ, Son of God, have mercy on me." According to personal need, this form was shortened, omitting one phrase of it or another. St. Gregory of Sinai (and Mt. Athos) added the words, "the sinner," *ton hamartolon.*[11a]

When the Jesus Prayer spread north into Slavonic lands, the Russian hesychasts came to like the long formula. St. Nilus of Sora (1443-1508) is known to have used and defended the use of the addition "a sinner." Thus the "old Slavonic" formula, in transliteration, is: *Gospodi Iisuse Christe, Suine Bojii, Pomilui mya greshnago.* That is, "Lord Jesus Christ, Son of God, have mercy on me, a sinner." This is the common formula among the Russian Christian people today. Some no longer use the old Slavonic form, but modern Russian, which runs: *Gospód Iisús Hristós, Sin Bójii, milostiv bud mne gréshnamu.*

For the sake of comparison:

(English)	(Greek)
Lord Jesus Christ	*Kýrie* Iesoú Christé
Son of God	Huié Theou
have mercy on me	*eléison* me.
(a sinner).	(ton hamartolón).

(Old Slavonic)	(Russian)
Góspodi Iisúse Christé	Gospód Iisús Hristós
Suíne Bójii (baw zhe)	Sin Bójii
Pomílui mya	milostív bud mne.
gréshnago.	gréshnomu.

The italicized words are familiar to us in the Eucharistic Liturgy: they form a variant of the Jesus Prayer.

Practice of The Jesus Prayer

The Jesus Prayer is usually associated with breathing . . . a rhythmic breathing. However, this process is merely an aid—granted, a very helpful one—and is not necessary for the prayer. In the beginning the attention to the breathing is decidedly helpful for relaxation and concentration. The ideal is to let the process do its work without demanding further attention, just as any acquired habit sets us free to attend to something more important.

As noted in the previous chapter on Centering Prayer, images and thoughts that are related to desires and fears will tend to tense us up, shorten our breath and tighten our muscles. In these circumstances it will be advantageous to make the effort to focus on the breathing and the prayer long enough to re-establish a rhythm and relaxation.

During the course of the prayer, if God should bestow the gift of infusion, the breathing becomes so quiet, gentle and unobtrusive that it almost seems to cease, as though we were not breathing at all.

In what follows, I have in mind that larger group of persons who might like to use the Jesus Prayer as *a* way, among others, for finding union with God. Except in a few cases, the Western-minded person is not likely to make this prayer *the* way he or she chooses for going to God. That will be more readily understood, I hope, after reading the section of this chapter, dealing with hesychasm.

Now, to exercise the Jesus Prayer with breathing will require at first a little experimentation. Obviously, it would be helpful to have the aid of an experienced hand if such a person is available. Inevitably questions arise. On the other hand, anyone who has already been exposed to Transcendental Meditation, Zen or Yoga, and who now wants to convert to the more directly Christian Jesus Prayer should find the change-over greatly facilitated, being already accustomed to using a mantra or koan in conjunction with the breathing process. (But let me emphasize that the Jesus Prayer is not merely a mantra or koan; rather, it is the invoking of a person whom we love or desire to love. It involves an I—Thou relationship.)

Let us work into the Prayer through the simplest form, namely, the Holy Name of Jesus. "Jesus" has two syllables: the first and accented syllable, *Je*; and the second and unaccented syllable, *sus*. Likewise, breathing has two motions: inhaling and exhaling.

As we inhale, we coordinate our quiet, relaxed and almost silent "pronunciation" of the accented syllable, *Jeeeeee*; and as we exhale, we tail-off with the unaccented syllable, *suuuuss*. While experimenting with this coordination of breathing and "pronunciation," we find that it is quite natural to breathe the word *Je-sus* in such a way that it is almost indistinguishable from the breathing, and with practically no forming of the word with the movement of tongue and mouth. Let it become a rhythm that loses sight of the syllables and becomes a flow as natural as the breathing. Thus, it becomes very soothing to the body, the mind and the heart. Jesus seems already to be a comforter just by the quiet saying of His Blessed Name.

With growing peace and restfulness, we find the Prayer becoming inaudible altogether, falling away into a silent, mental "pronunciation" of the Holy Name. And as in Centering Prayer, we may reach a point of stillness, with the prayer becoming a silent, loving presence. Thus the Name of Jesus becomes completely interiorized, and heart meets heart.

In any prayer period, then, the movement of the prayer goes through a normal evolution, starting out as a breathed, whispered *vocal* prayer, involving lips, tongue and throat muscles. It soon becomes simplified to a prayer of the *mind*, and then hopefully, slips inside the cloister of the *heart* to find him to whom we belong.

Father Kallistos has called my attention to the fact that the use of the Holy Name alone is not common practice among the Orthodox. He himself does not recommend less than "Lord Jesus," *Kyrie Iesou*, for he feels the Holy Name by itself is too powerful, too concentrated. Perhaps there are some rare birds like myself who will find the Name alone the most suitable form of the Invocation. Some experimentation seems to be necessary for everyone.

Now if we should decide to try the full formula of the Jesus Prayer, what do we do? Let's take the formula: "Lord Jesus Christ, Son of God, have mercy on me, a sinner." In the beginning it may not be easy to say the whole invocation within the limits of one inhalation and exhalation. Nor is that necessarily the most effective way to use the invocation even after we have acquired a facility to "make it fit." What is important is the slow, restful, attentive, prayerful use of the words so as to be drawn in sympathy and love to the abiding shepherd of our heart.

Under these circumstances, it is wise to divide the Prayer formula into its four meaningful components. As we inhale, we say or "breathe" the words: *Lord Jesus Christ*. As we exhale, we breathe out the words: *Son of God* (or "Son of the Living God" if it means more to us; or even "Son of the Father"). On the next inhalation we breathe: *have mercy on me*. And exhaling, we breathe: *a sinner* (or if we are a "bug" on balance: "a sinner, a sinner").

In the East it is the more common practice to breathe in while praying: "Lord Jesus Christ, Son of God," and to breathe out with "have mercy on me (a sinner)."

The revelation, the theology, the thought content implied

in the full invocation is abundant. Like the mysteries of the
rosary, it can nourish the mind of the beginner admirably.
Nevertheless, it is good to realize that ultimately prayer's home
is in the heart.

No one should miss the treat of reading *The Way of a
Pilgrim*.[12] That saintly pilgrim of the last century who jour-
neyed about Russia, reciting the Jesus Prayer 12,000 times per
day[13] arrived at a very deep level of union with God. But this
raises the question, "Should I try to say the Jesus Prayer a
certain number of times per day, like that stout-hearted young
man?" He must have been reciting the full formula at something like every five seconds over the whole course of the day.
This could cause great tension. Another Russian, Bishop Ignatius Brianchaninov, advised beginning with a hundred invocations per day, recited slowly and with full attention.[14] He
considered a half-hour as about the time needed to accomplish
this, which would amount to a single invocation about every
fifteen to twenty seconds. As we have the time, he advised
adding on by a hundred, but never burdening ourselves with
quantity, and never at the expense of hurrying through the
invocation of the Holy Name. A gradual increase avoids tension.

It is important to realize that if we are experiencing the
building up of tension, we are more than likely doing something incorrectly, and it is for our well-being to locate the
source of the problem. Unreasonable effort and over-enthusi-
asm are frequently involved.

We stand to benefit from an American Cistercian's experience:

> About ten years ago I read the fascinating story of the
> Russian peasant who assiduously practiced the Jesus-
> Prayer. The book was entitled "The Way of the Pilgrim,"
> ... The account so gripped me that even before I finished
> the book I started using the Jesus-Prayer. With all the other
> prayers, readings, etc., of the pre-Vatican II days, I still
> managed to say the Prayer over 5000 times daily. But after a
> few weeks of that I informed my confessor that I was either
> going to be a mystic or a maniac. Then I wrote a letter to

Tom Merton explaining my situation. In his reply he
warned me that we Americans cannot adopt Russian spirituality without modification, and that I should curtail my
saying the Prayer.[15]

This account shows the wisdom of acting when tension
arises and the need of seeking the advice and aid of others more
experienced and better informed than ourselves.

Thomas Merton mentioned the necessity of making modi-
fications in using the Prayer. This is precisely what the Russians themselves did according to their circumstances. The
following passage by a good spiritual director (staretz), the
famous Ambrose of Optino, written to a prioress, relates some
interesting details surrounding the devout Pilgrim and gives us
some appropriate counseling in prayer:

> This manuscript was written by a peasant from the prov-
> ince of Orel who was taught the Prayer of Jesus by an
> unknown staretz. You write that the manuscript of this
> peasant ends in 1859. Shortly before that time we heard
> from our late staretz, Father Macarius, that he was visited
> by a layman who had attained to such a high degree of
> spiritual prayer that Fr. Macarius could only tell him: "Be
> humble, be humble." Afterwards he told us about this
> experience with astonishment.... I shall tell you in a few
> words of the manuscript of the pilgrim. There is nothing
> objectionable in it. The pilgrim lived as a pilgrim. He was a
> wanderer, free from cares and worries. He could freely
> practice prayer when he wanted. But you lead the life of a
> prioress and, besides, you are sickly, hardened with monas-
> tic duties. Therefore practice prayer as much as you are free
> to, and the rest will be made up for by obedience which also
> has its importance.[16]

Returning to our American Cistercian monk, we have
something more to learn from him. After his first experience
with the Jesus Prayer he eventually was exposed to TM and to
other Eastern techniques for meditating. This led him back
again to the Jesus Prayer in a way that now fits him and
benefits him. He describes his procedure this way:

For a formal meditation, I go to a quiet, solitary place, and take up a relaxed sitting position. Closing the eyes, I concentrate my full attention on the eyelids. This is a sensitive area, so one can perceive readily if any tension or constriction is present. I tell myself to relax the eyelids, and find that, empathetically, the jaw and whole face loosen up. Then I slowly mention the other parts of the body, giving them a second or two to relax: neck, shoulders, chest, waist, thighs, legs, feet. This is merely a preliminary exercise, designed to grant the body its recognition, and to bring it to a state of tranquility. When one ignores the simple laws and needs of the body, he finds that the body has ways of "getting back," even during the meditation (in antics such as coughing, scratching, squirming, itching...). Respect Brother Body, and he will respect you!

When the body is completely relaxed, I start the countdown exercise. Beginning with ten, I count down to one very slowly, saying the numbers interiorly: 10 - 9 - 8 - 7. Here I pause to say, "I am going down deeper and deeper," continuing with, 6 - 5 - 4. Again I stop to say "deeper and deeper," then finishing with, 3 - 2 - 1. At this point a deep calm has come over me, interiorly as well as exteriorly. (This would be confirmed by an electroencephalograph, as the Alpha state.)

Now I let the Jesus Prayer come on of itself. My chosen formula is "CHRIST—MERCY." I purposely reduced the ordinary longer formula because it was easier to use as a mantra. I opted for only two words, for they can easily be accommodated to the breathing process, inhaling on "CHRIST" and exhaling on "MERCY." For a few minutes I breathe the prayer in this manner. As this continues, the breathing becomes slower, until it is hardly noticeable, with the words also getting fainter, more refined. My eyes are always kept closed, whether the meditation is for ten minutes or an hour.

After a few minutes of the prayer in unison with the breath, I then relax any conscious control. Either the prayer will continue to be coupled with the breath, or (as more usually happens) I find myself simply repeating the one word "CHRIST" ever so softly, protractedly. It is at this deep interior level that sometimes the word "CHRIST" fades out, leaving me in a sort of felt-immedi-acy of the Person of Jesus; not that there is any clear perception, as by an image, but by experiential faith I am consciously aware of his Sacred Presence. At those mo-ments I just keep still, content to be with him, neither thinking nor saying anything. Thus the prayer-mantra has accomplished its work, leading me into the felt-presence of the Mysterious One, the Personal Reality behind the Name.

Alas, these precious moments of "enlightenment" are not too frequent (no doubt due to my unclean, sinful condition; also indicating that more purification is due). When I be-come aware that some other image, fantasy, idea has surrep-titiously crept into my field of interior awareness, that is a signal for a return to a gentle repetition of the mantra.[17]

In the closing paragraphs he offers an interesting solution to the problem of sleepiness during the meditation:

When I am making this prayer for a longer period of time, there comes the moment when I notice that I am getting sleepy. To counteract this, I lie down on the floor on my back, completely stretched out. I let all my limbs and mem-bers go completely limp, and stay in this position for a minute or two. From actual experience I have found that this short "giving in" has the actual effect of a longer nap. Then after a minute or two, I return to my chair and the prayer. It is only rarely that sleep will try to creep up on me after that "exercise."

And then he encourages the use of the Jesus Prayer during the activities of daily living, not limiting it to formal prayer periods:

One final remark: with the Jesus-mantra, one is joyfully encouraged to use the mantra all during the day. In fact, the more one uses it, the easier will it be to "meditate" with it. Of course, used "not as the gentiles do," with vain repeti-tion, but said with faith and some degree of attentiveness to his Presence: whether one is working, driving a car, eating, walking, taking a shower, recreating—any human activity.

This captivating personal account enables us to share in a less formidable and much more interesting way the many details connected with this form of praying. Also, we cannot help noticing in these details the many similarities with Centering Prayer in the previous chapter. This enables us to see that any technique leading to contemplative prayer is going to show strong resemblances to its brothers and sisters in West and East, in regard to the essentials of the technique.

Related Comments

Eastern Christians, when beginning to practice the Jesus Prayer, are known to use a cord or a kind of rosary of a hundred knots or beads in order to have the body involved in their praying and to aid attention. The prayer cord is helpful up to that point where the mind—and the Prayer—enter the heart, and the fingering of knots or beads fades away and becomes impossible. "Counting" invocations is only an inducement to bring us to Jesus himself.[17a]

My own experience of the Jesus Prayer has been two-fold. In regard to prayer periods, it has never for long displaced for me the way of *lectio divina*. But as an accompaniment during other activities of the day, it has been a treasured help. In an attempt to use it to foster unceasing prayer, I would use a rosary, which was noisy as Western rosaries tend to be and which was forever getting tangled and demanding more unceasing patience than aiding unceasing prayer. In the farm shop one afternoon I found a bearing in the "damaged parts" box. I slipped my ring-finger into the inner race of the bearing and spun the outer race with a flip of my thumb. "That should do it," I thought. And it did.

The bearing can't get tangled; it doesn't rattle and rustle; it is compact (the outer race measures a quarter-inch in width and one and three-eighths inches in diameter); and by running it on to my ring-finger I still have the use of my forefinger and thumb which was not the case with a rosary that seemed to be forever escaping through the least opening in my covering fist.

But best of all I liked the bearing because it eliminated the tendency to count beads, and who wants to count the flips of a revolving bearing! I didn't want to know whether I prayed the Holy Name ten times or a hundred times in an hour ... it didn't matter.[18]

One of the "occupational hazards" I experience as a monk who listens to many Liturgical readings each day at community prayer is my wandering attention, especially if the reading does not strike me as very interesting. I happened on to a solution suggested by Bishop Brianchaninov who advised the use of the Jesus Prayer during "church services" to keep the mind centered on the "singing and reading."[19] At first I thought this would be a distraction from the readings, until I tried it and discovered that he was right. Breathing silently the solitary word "Jesus" fosters alertness and concentration.

Before closing section one, it may be of benefit to point out that the bishop mentions several material aids aside from, or in addition to, the breathing and use of a prayer cord: he speaks of a somewhat darkened room for the prayer period, of keeping the eyes closed, and of alternating full prostrations and bows to the waist as one recites the Jesus Prayer.[20] He immediately discusses the danger of delusion in the use of material supports insofar as many people seem to use them imprudently, and find satisfaction in success which is not real success.[21]

He is seconded in this by another bishop, Theophan the Recluse, who goes even further and warns that the prayer is not a talisman. There is no value even in the words of the prayer in themselves and apart from an attitude of soul which seeks the loving remembrance of God and union of mind and heart with him.[22]

This should serve to remind us that the Jesus Prayer or any other way of prayer does not assure us of automatic success. As Father Kallistos points out, "There is no mechanical technique, whether physical or mental, which can compel God to manifest his presence. His grace is conferred always as a free gift, and cannot be gained automatically by any method or techique."[22a] A right attitude, a right focus is essential. And when these methods are said to make prayer "easy," this should

be taken in a relative sense.[23] We may recall in Chapter Four
Abba Agathon saying that prayer is a warfare. And Bishop
Brianchaninov called it a "hidden martyrdom."[24]

But for anyone who is willing to pay the price of true love:

> The door of the invisible world opens before him and he
> enters into many mansions. And once he enters these man-
> sions, the doors of others open before him. If he entered a
> hundred mansions, the doors of another hundred would
> open. He is continually enriched. The more he is enriched,
> the more are the wonders revealed to him. To him, as to the
> son and heir, God entrusts that which cannot be appre-
> hended by human nature or expressed by word.[25]

Hesychasm and The Jesus Prayer

The Hesychasm (from *hesychia*, meaning inner and outer
tranquility; associated with the solitary life) which flourished
as a medieval Orthodox movement was and is a lineal descendent of the spirituality of the Desert Fathers. St. John Climacus
through his *Ladder*[26] could be designated a principal bridge
(along with Diadochus, Isaac of Syria, Hesychius and others)
connecting the early solitaries with the solitaries of famous Mt.
Athos.

In "rung" 27 of the *Ladder*, St. John teaches a holy solitude
(*hesychia*) of body and soul. What does the solitary attempt to
do? He tries to contain his everyday life within his own body!
As far as possible he closes up his activity within the bound-
aries of himself for the kingdom is present within. It is truly a
radical existence. It requires no small psychic and spiritual
maturity before daring to launch upon such a life project and
life style. St. John says that a man lacking this maturity and
attempting such a life is as good as a man jumping from the
safety of a ship into the sea and expecting to ride ashore on a
sinking plank. He chooses his words carefully: "Angelic
strength is needed for the solitary life. I speak of those who
lead a life of real solitude of body and soul."[27]

The solitary chooses a life of severe asceticism and depriva-
tion as an inevitable consequence of his aim. He will lack some
of the "necessities" of life, and this will be a test for his

perseverance. But Climacus speaks assuringly that the great fruit of this perseverance will be converse with the Lord as face to face in the depths of the heart.

To achieve such an ambition however, he must, so to say, take a seat on a high place and scrutinize carefully the kinds of thieves who are trying to get into the heart. He becomes a man of fiber, of deep spiritual strength. He becomes a man *par excellence* of listening within, of alertness, awareness; a guardian of the heart. He becomes a man of great desire, continual *metanoia*, compunction, radical poverty; of "defencelessness" and total *fiat*; silent of lips and heart, with a holy dispassionateness and detachment ... surrounded and impregnated with divine faith and charity. He willingly bears the cross of temptation and of the sense of abandonment, but not within the accompaniment of sighs, groans and weeping. He is grateful for his life and call; he adores and he loves with a compassionate love, both the suffering Christ and his fellow men.

Continual prayer is the heart of hesychasm, and for St. John, the hesychast's strength is linked to the abundance and depth of his prayer. It is the mindfulness of Jesus "present with each breath" that sustains him and teaches him the value of *hesychia*.[28]

Fearing a breach in prayer, the Saint advises manual work only as an aid to overcome the drowsiness after a midday nap ... or perhaps he means to ward off the taking of a midday nap. He esteems holy reading, but as soon as it touches off prayer he considers reading superfluous. He says that most of the night hours ought to be spent in prayer, as much as can be sustained, and only the remainder should be devoted to reciting the psalms. The same applies to the daylight hours.

For persons who are not ready for or fit for such a demanding life, it would be sheer folly to venture into it: "They waste time in being taken captive, robbed, made despondent and subjected to distraction"[29]

For certain they will be attached by the "demon of *acedia*." All solitaries are. But those who are spiritually mature resist and come away stronger for their wrestling, whereas, the others have little hope of remaining in their cells. Evagrius of Scete describes this struggle from his personal experience with great sharpness:

The demon of *acedia*—also called the noonday demon—is the one that causes the most serious trouble of all. He presses his attack upon the monk about the fourth hour [midmorning] and besieges the soul until the eighth hour [midafternoon]. First of all he makes it seem that the sun barely moves, if at all, and that the day is fifty hours long. Then he constrains the monk to look constantly out the windows, to walk outside the cell, to gaze carefully at the sun to determine how far it stands from the ninth hour [the hour for a daily meal], to look now this way and now that to see if perhaps (one of the brethren appears from his cell). Then too he instills in the heart of the monk a hatred for the place, a hatred for his very life itself, a hatred for manual labor. He leads him to reflect that charity has departed from among the brethren, that there is no one to give encouragement. Should there be someone at this period who happens to offend him in some way or other, this too the demon uses to contribute further to his hatred. This demon drives him along to desire other sites where he can more easily procure life's necessities, more readily find work and make a real success of himself. He goes on to suggest that, after all, it is not the place that is the basis of pleasing the Lord. God is to be adored everywhere. He joins to these reflections the memory of his dear ones and of his former way of life. He depicts life stretching out for a long period of time, and brings before the mind's eye the toil of the ascetic struggle and, as the saying has it, leaves no leaf unturned to induce the monk to forsake his cell and drop out of the fight. No other demon follows close upon the heels of this one (when he is defeated) but only a state of deep peace and inexpressible joy arise out of this struggle.[30]

The Abba Philemon is an example of the accomplished hesychast. His disciple self-appointedly decided to test him by neglecting to bring him his bread for several days, which was the sum of his nourishment besides salt and water. The Abba was so preoccupied with his prayer that he never inquired why his bread did not appear. On another occasion, the disciple had to take ship from Alexandria to Constantinople and was away for a considerable time without telling Philemon where or why he was going. Upon his return, the Abba beamed with joy at seeing him, but never asked why, where or what he had done.

Inquiring about this silence, the disciple got the response, "From the time I came to the skete I would not let my thought go beyond the walls of my cell, ..."[31]

Living in step with this tradition, the holy Nicephorus the Hesychast and his contemporary, St. Gregory of Sinai (1255-1346), were instrumental in reviving the mystical movement among the monks of Mt. Athos and even further afield. This spirituality made such a "hit" that many who were unable to go into physical solitude gave themselves over to living as "spiritual" hesychasts.

Nicephorus was one of those who spread the technique of "navel-gazing" which hostile circles misunderstood and which brought a good thing into disrepute. Nicephorus himself knew what he was about and his method worked for him. Unfortunately, many inexperienced hands tried the same and failed to benefit—even to the point of wrecking their health and their sanity. Many later writers, including Bishop Brianchaninov and Theophan the Recluse, toned down the method, both in their description of it and in advising its use. (We have already gotten a hint of this at the close of section one of this chapter.)

Hesychia literally means stillness, quiet, tranquillity. And specifically and interiorly it means guarding the heart so as to have the constant remembrance of God and the possession of inner prayer. This is the central consideration both of the Desert Fathers and the later hesychasts.[32]

Nicephorus was no exception. He fully accepted this and strove to achieve this goal in his own life. He either inherited or devised an intensive (to put it mildly) technique for "keeping his mind fixed in his heart." He thought of breathing as a natural way to the heart, and so he says, "Having collected your mind within you, lead it into the channel of breathing through which air reaches the heart and, together with this inhaled air, force your mind to descend into the heart and to remain there."[33] (His physiology was "off," but his purpose was "on.") He sympathized with the feeling of imprisonment and loneliness which anyone experiences who tries to succeed at this practice for long periods. But he goes on to encourage the constant use of the Jesus Prayer with breathing to maintain this centeredness.

This is where the low stool comes into the picture, and the

chin pressed against the breast; the curling up in a kind of foetal position with the eyes fixed about where the navel is; and the holding of breath to keep the mind in the heart and making it stay there. No wonder complaints were heard of inexperienced people wrecking their health and sanity. This was a total dedication to prayer which "totalled" the imprudent. But the method was sound for the person who knew what he was really trying to achieve. To restrain the wandering eye, especially the eye of curiosity, by fixing the gaze—as we do even today with a candle flame, an icon or a crucifix, etc.—and to attempt even by bodily symbolism to gather all of oneself into the heart in posture, motion and breathing ... all of this was aimed at discovering the life of the spirit and the many mansioned kingdom within.

Archimandrite Kallistos brings all of this together as follows:

> Inward stillness, when interpreted as a guarding of the heart and a return into oneself, implies a passage from multiplicity to unity, from diversity to simplicity and spiritual poverty. To use the terminology of Evagrius, the mind must become "naked." This aspect of *hesychia* is made explicit in another definition provided by St. John Climacus: "*hesychia* is a laying aside of thoughts." Here he is adapting an Evagrian phrase, "Prayer is a laying aside of thoughts." *Hesychia* involves a progressive self-emptying, in which the mind is stripped of all visual images and man-made concepts, and so contemplates in purity the realm of God. The hesychast, from this point of view, is one who has advanced from *praxis* to *theoria*, from the active to the contemplative life. St. Gregory of Sinai contrasts the hesychast with the *praktikos*, and goes on to speak of " ... the hesychasts who are content to pray to God alone within their heart and to abstain from thoughts." The hesychast, then, is not so much one who refrains from meeting and speaking with others, as one who in his life of prayer renounces all images, words and discursive reasoning, who is "lifted above the senses into pure silence."
>
> ... The hesychast ceases from his own activity, not in order to be idle, but in order to enter into the activity of God.[34]

It should be becoming clear why Orthodox writers warn against venturing into the hesychastic style of life without having a spiritual director (a *staretz* of *hegumen* or *abba*) to whom is openly revealed one's temptations, motives, aims, intentions, and the like (*starchestvo* or "manifestation of conscience"). The dangers are fairly obvious: intolerable tensions involving health, both physical and psychological, not to mention spiritual insofar as one who ends as a failure will for all his efforts also not find the union with God he was expecting or presuming.

But do not most of these same writers caution that anyone who takes up the Jesus Prayer ought also to have guidance? Why is that? Certainly no one could reasonably deny that a good director would be a treasurable aid for any method of prayer or spiritual life style. Spiritual direction is the more crucial depending on the inexperience of the person and the demands of the prayer or life style concerned.

If, for example, we are talking in terms of taking up the Jesus Prayer as a pious aspiration which we would like to say occasionally, looking it up in a book will suffice. But if we are thinking of a serious use of the prayer to add to our other ways of seeking union with God, some spiritual advice might save us a little wasted effort and initial confusion; nevertheless we will probably do all right on our own unless we lack common sense to a considerable degree. On the other hand, to launch into the Jesus Prayer as our way, *the* way, is the same as saying we make or break over this. We better have a director! There is too much at stake and too many ways of going awry.

Only after the passions have been brought under control can anyone safely profit from his solitude. Also, the Fathers advise against an arrogant man becoming a solitary, for self-will will bring him to a bad end. And the person who cannot trust or surrender himself to the guidance of a director is likewise in danger of ending up warped and distorted. The Staretz Zosima elaborates this point:

> The enemy, knowing full well how deadly is the custom of keeping everything to oneself, encourages and inspires the ascetic to live on without revealing his thoughts. He who has accepted such a devilish inspiration is deluded, thinking

that he lives well and without sin in his relation with the
staretz, while he is not frank in hiding his thoughts. Therefore he does not feel peace and consolation in his soul.
Because he lives with his Staretz without faith and love he
is overcome with murmuring, pride, condemnation of others, dissatisfaction and absence of peace. These spiritual
illnesses, fortified by being hidden, make the life with the
Staretz intolerable. They go so far as to force this man to
leave his Father and the brotherhood. Seduced by his self-
will and his own wisdom, such a man abandons the right
road approved by the Holy Fathers.[35]

We see the benefits of openness in the following passage:

To aid the soul in its exercises, and to preserve its balance,
continuous guidance is necessary. Such guidance makes
uninterrupted progress toward perfection possible, without
the spiritual fluctuations and vicissitudes common to people who have no guide. There is needed someone who
knows the soul, its dispositions, abilities and sins, a person
with spiritual experience and wisdom, one who can guide
the soul, encouraging it in times of laziness and sadness and
restraining it in times of immoderate elation, one who
knows how to humble pride, foresee danger and treat sins
with penance. Quick and safe is the way of the man who
has subjected himself to such guidance because he practices
then two great virtues: obedience and humility. Manifestation of conscience which is the condition *sine qua non* of
starchestvo, is a powerful means of progress, terrible to the
enemy of our salvation. The unrevealed thought troubles
and depresses the soul; revealed, it falls away and does no
harm.[36]

By way of concluding this chapter, the task of the hesy-
chast/Jesus Prayer devotee may be seen in the light of
Theophan's teaching: "The term *Vnutr-prebuivanie*, staying
within, means strictly speaking a conscious centering in the
heart, an intense, gathering thereto of all the forces of soul and
body...."[37] This involves trying to center all feeling and the
whole affective makeup of our being, as well as mind and will,
in the heart. It is an attempt to come to the point where all of
one's being is saying *yes* to God.

But God also has his ever-faithful part to play. He draws and attracts and reveals himself even as the purification of feeling, mind and will takes place. The early phases (when the hesychast doesn't "have it all together" yet) are a discovering of the Lord in the meeting place of the heart, but as meeting with him face to face at midnight in the bottom of a dry well. Or, if you prefer, meeting him covered with a thick impenetrable veil. The veil gradually thins and melts away as love intensifies. As in every spiritual way he invites us to himself through the daily deaths that are continually preparing us for the final one, and the life beyond. The victory is expressed in the words of a hesychast responding to the question, "Father, what do you think of death?"

> "There is no death," he answered, "there is merely a passing from one state to another. To me personally, the life of the other world is much more real than my life here. . . . The more the Christian lives the interior life, the more he is detached from this world, and imperceptibly he approaches the other world. When the end comes it is easy; the thin veil simply dissolves. . . ."[38]

Psalms 130 and 72 must have been meant especially for the hesychast; they express his life so well:

> Truly I have set my soul
> in silence and peace. (130:2)

> I was always in your presence;
> you were holding me by my right hand.
> You will guide me by your counsel
> and so you will lead me to glory.

> What else have I in heaven but you?
> Apart from you I want nothing on earth.
> My body and my heart faint for joy;
> You, my God, are my possession for ever.

> . . .

> To be near God is my happiness
> I have made the Lord God my refuge.
> I will tell of all your works . . . (72: 23-26,28. Grail)

Chapter Ten

The Way of Lectio Divina

Lectio divina is response to a call to communion with the Word of the Father. The Word leads us back time and again to the Father from whom we are continually straying by the forgetfulness of trivial fascinations, emotional attachments, mental preoccupations and moral "escapades."

As response, *lectio divina* is a reading, a listening to God's great book of Revelation. It is a listening to the Word behind His revealed word which we read in private, or hear read by another in the liturgical gatherings. We meet the Word speaking to us in the words of a homilist or in the colloquy of a spiritual friend. In the first days of Christianity the "Good News" was not in print, but was a living Person. After the drama of Pentecost the Apostles and disciples conveyed Him to others by preaching, and only later was He "reduced" to the written page. Even then, due to the shortage of copies, the word of God, the word of salvation was proclaimed publicly by a reader, or lector, in the assembly of the Faithful. Private reading was only possible with the multiplication of handwritten texts. But the more the copies multiplied the more was *lectio divina* thought of in its narrowest sense of private reading.

In a much more loose and analogous sense, *lectio divina* might also be taken as a listening to God's other imposing "book," that of Creation. In this case we catch sight of the Word in nature, where he stands behind the soundless return

114

of the rising sun and the silent *adieu* of its setting, and the slow march of constellations night after night and generation to generation. We hear the divine voice in the clamor of the cricket and the katydid, and the funny croaking of the bull frog. He speaks to us out of the gift of every meal, every breath we breathe, and our repose in sleep.

The Word wants to be heard and recognized in every daily gift. But what is every gift without the gift of the giver himself, from whose open side we ourselves have come, and to whom we belong?

Indeed the giver is a Divine Lover. His is a call to communion. He courts a beloved for whom he paid the price of his life's blood. The beloved is the Church and each member of the Church from the bridal Mother of God to the least of the *anawim*. This is the beautiful teaching of the Scriptures and of long Christian tradition. Thus *lectio divina* has an offerer and a recipient. It is a relationship—a relationship of love/prayer/communion.

Lectio divina is a way of light and love (in contrast with *The Cloud of Unknowing* which is a way of darkness and love). *Lectio divina* begins with an eager seeking of the Word in his revealed word, the seeking of truth in his established truth; it begins with searching out the charms of the divine bridegroom from Genesis to the final cry "Come! Lord Jesus."

The truths and charms of the lover captivate the beloved's attention, and they become like so many blandishments that play upon the heart-strings. As though serenaded by the wonders of this Divine Betrothed, the beloved tries to respond with ardent darts of affection and love-sick praises and thanksgivings. Then the day comes when the Lover's revealed beauty reduces the bride to awe-struck silence and ecstatic love. *Lectio* culminates in a mystic embrace.

Recall from the closing pages of Chapter Six how *lectio divina* may be taken either in a limited sense as sacred reading only, or in the fuller sense as a process of prayer escalation or intensification involving *lectio, meditatio, oratio,* and *contemplatio*. In the present chapter we are interested in this fuller meaning of *lectio divina*. We will: (1) look at some monastic accounts of this practice; (2) provide a practical procedure; (3) elaborate on that procedure; and (4) consider the four elements in turn.

Some Historical Background

Although *lectio divina* is a vital part of the Benedictine-Cistercian tradition, it did not have its origin with St. Benedict, but is common to all monasticism.

In the life of St. Antony, the great solitary and Father of Monasticism, for example, it is said that he taught his imitators in the ascetic life to be satisfied with the Sacred Scriptures as sufficient for their reading and study.[1] He urged them to commit to memory all of the commandments and instructions of the Scriptures; and he cautioned them, "whatever you do, do it according to the testimony of the Sacred Scriptures."[2] As for himself in his youth, we are told that "he was so attentive to the reading of the Scripture lessons that nothing escaped him; he retained everything and so his memory served him in place of books."[3] The famous account of his conversion to the ascetic life mentions how he was meditating on his way to Church, reflecting that the apostles left everything for Christ and that the post-Pentecost converts sold their possessions and distributed to the poor and needy through the hands of the apostles. As he stepped into the assembly, the Gospel of the rich young man was being read, and he heard the words: "If you will be perfect, go sell all that you have ... and come, follow me. ..." He received the message as if meant particularly for him, and after the liturgy he went out and acted upon it.[4]

He then gave himself over to intense private prayer to satisfy the exhortation to pray without ceasing. He visited the ascetics in the neighborhood of his village to listen to their words of advice and holy teaching, and he would leave, determined to practice the outstanding quality of each of them. In one he observed a devotion to study; in another, the faithful keeping of a nightly vigil; and in a third, constancy in his prayer.[5] He treasured the Psalms and knew them by heart, and he recited them daily. "Day by day he sighed as he meditated on the heavenly mansions."[6]

Although he had no formal schooling (he knew no Greek, nor Greek literature and philosophers) he was nevertheless recognized later in life as a man of urbanity whose speech was seasoned with divine wisdom.[7] His many disciples covered the desert hills with their cells. They were "like tents filled with divine choirs—singing Psalms, studying, . . . praying, rejoicing in the hope of the life to come."[8]

St. Pachomius required his cenobites to be literate. He also required that they read and memorize the New Testament; and especially to learn the whole Psalter of 150 Psalms. St. Basil was much of the same mind in regard to his monks. St. Jerome, as we saw in Chapter Four, advised the young Rusticus to read Scripture industriously and love that sacred word, and to learn the Psalms word for word.

St. Benedict, the great legislator of Western monasticism, established in his Rule a special time for each day when the monks were to give themselves over assiduously to *lectio/oratio*. The time varied throughout the year according to the season— be it harvest season or Lent, etc.—from a daily total of about 2 1/2 hours to 5 hours, which indicates the importance attached to it.

The content of their reading/reflection/prayer was primarily Sacred Scripture and then the commentaries and teachings of the Fathers on Scripture (for example, St. Cyprian, St. Ambrose, Augustine and Jerome) and the Lives and the Sayings of the Fathers as found in St. Athanasius' life of Antony and in Cassian's Conferences and Institutes, as well as the writings of St. Basil, whom Benedict mentions by name.

Mindful of the monastic East, St. Benedict prescribed prolonged reading of the Scriptures by his monks (chapter 48). He also prescribed their listening to the readings mentioned above at specified times in the day such as the "lessons" at the hours of the Divine Office, the reading in the dining room while the monks ate, and at the close of the day at the pre-Compline reading. It was already tradition that the monks' private reading, and even the public readings, should be accompanied by careful pondering, "chewing the cud for all its worth." Benedict also encouraged the various modes of spontaneous *oratio*: the short bursts of ardent prayer mentioned among the Desert Fathers, along with prayer accompanied by silent tears, and Cassian's "prayer of fire."

What lay behind this intense life of *lectio, meditatio, oratio* and *contemplatio* as urged by St. Benedict? His exhortation in

the prologue of his Rule is right in line with the youthful
Antony attentive to the voice of Jesus speaking to the rich
young man. "Listen, my son, to . . . the Master and . . . comply
with the admonition of your loving Father . . . the Lord Jesus
Christ our true King. . . . And our eyes being opened to the
deifying light, let us listen with wondering ears. . . ." Benedict
puts the question of the Psalmist in the mouth of Jesus, "Who
is the man who will have life and desires to see good days?"
And if you respond, "Count me in!," Our Lord ends his invitation and counsel with the consoling words, "Before you call
upon me, 'Behold I am present.'" And Benedict concludes,
"What, dearest brethren, can be sweeter than this voice of the
Lord inviting us? Behold how in his loving kindness he shows
us the way of life."

The holy legislator labeled his monastery a "school of the
Lord's service." St. Bernard enhanced this expression of love
and life by calling the monastery a "school of charity." The
Cistercians were clearly in the mainstream of the monastic
tradition of *lectio divina*.

The Benedictine Abbot William of St. Thierry (before he
himself became a Cistercian) was so impressed with St. Bernard's Abbey of Clairvaux that he remarked colorfully, "There
were tracks freshly made by men of our own day in the path
that had first been trodden by our fathers, the Egyptian monks
of long ago."[9] And of St. Bernard, William says, "It was his
great delight to pass hours in reading Scripture."[10] He elaborates:

> While he worked, his prayer and holy thoughts went on
> uninterrupted. . . . Even to this day he will claim that it was
> by praying and meditating in the woods and fields that he
> discovered the deep meaning of Holy Writ. During the
> hours that were not devoted to manual labor, he either read,
> or prayed, or meditated. If he had a chance to be alone he
> would use it for prayer . . . He used to tell us that he found
> it easier to understand the text of Scripture itself than
> lengthy explanations of it. But even so he did read the old
> commentaries of the Fathers . . . And like them he drank
> avidly of the one fountain, which is Holy Writ. Since he has
> become so intimately acquainted with the text of Scripture,
> he is filled with the same Spirit who inspired its writers . . .

And as he preaches and bases his sermons on scriptural
texts, he makes the passage so clear and moving that anyone
versed at all in secular or spiritual learning cannot help
marveling at the words he speaks.[11]

We have the testimony of St. Bernard's younger contemporary St. Aelred of Rievaulx, voicing in his own behalf what
St. Antony had advised his disciples eight centuries earlier
regarding the chosen pre-eminence of the biblical writings:

In the monastery, the Scriptures constituted the total of my
reading. The more I read Scripture, the less was I inclined
toward reading that was not permeated by the odor of
Scripture. A test came when I again took up Cicero's little
book and found it, too, had lost favor with me. Why?
Because it lacked Christ's name. I knew now that for the
future what lacked this sweet influence would have no
power to please me.[12]

In this passage, Aelred states clearly why he was being
drawn to the Holy Scriptures. Another disciple of Bernard,
Blessed Guerric, Abbot of Igny, has the same mind and urges
his monks to search the Scriptures: "For you are not mistaken
in thinking that you find life in them, you seek nothing else in
them but Christ to whom the Scriptures bear witness." He is
eager for his monks to keep "searching each and every word
like busy bees gathering honey from flowers," with the assurance that they will "reap the Spirit from the words."[13] Guerric
then puts the words of Sirach in the mouth of Jesus, "For my
Spirit is sweeter than honey and my inheritance surpasses the
honeycomb."[14]

Returning to William of St. Thierry (writing now as a
Cistercian monk in the Abbey of Signy), we can watch him
sketch the whole process of *lectio divina*. He takes up reading or
lectio first. With many years of personal experience behind him,
he advises scheduled hours for reading as well as scheduled
authors:

At fixed hours time should be given to certain definite
reading. For haphazard reading, constantly varied and as if
lighted upon by chance ... makes the mind unstable; ....

But you should concentrate on certain [scriptural] authors
and let your mind grow accustomed to them.[15]

He then remarks on the care to be given to the reading and
the need to enter the mind and meaning of the author through
persistent effort:

> The Scriptures need to be read and understood in the same
> spirit in which they were written. You will never enter into
> Paul's meaning until by constant application to reading him
> and by giving yourself to constant meditation you have
> imbibed his spirit. You will never understand David until
> by experience you have made the very sentiments of the
> psalms your own. And that applies to all Scripture.[16]

William now turns to *meditatio* or *ruminatio* which should
bring the reading to bear in personal application to one's own
life and vocation:

> Some part of your daily reading should also each day be
> committed to memory, taken in as it were into the stomach,
> to be more carefully digested and brought up again for
> frequent rumination; something in keeping with your voca-
> tion and helpful to concentration, something that will take
> hold of the mind and save it from distraction.[17]

Oratio is next, which William sees as not only not disrupt-
ing reading but a way of reaping the fruit of the reading and
engaging one more profoundly with it:

> The reading should also stimulate the feelings *(affectus)* and
> give rise to prayer, which should interrupt your reading: an
> interruption which should not so much hamper the reading
> as restore to it a mind more purified for understanding.[18]

William leaves no doubt that *lectio* shares in the act of
prayer by the intention of seeking God and the desire to meet
him in his written word and to bear fruit in his service:

> For reading serves the purpose of the intention with which
> it is done. If the reader truly seeks God in his reading,

everything that he reads tends to promote that end, making the mind surrender in the course of the reading and bring all that is understood into Christ's service.[19]

Finally, William speaks of *contemplatio* in terms of love, tasting God, the gaze of the spirit, awareness of God in joy and the deep experience of his goodness:

> When the object of thought is God and the things which relate to God and the will reaches the stage at which it becomes love, the Holy Spirit, the Spirit of life, at once infuses himself by way of love and gives life to everything, lending his assistance in prayer, in meditation or in study to man's weakness. Immediately the memory becomes wisdom and tastes with relish the good things of the Lord, while the thoughts to which they gave rise are brought to the intellect to be formed into affections. The understanding of the one thinking becomes the contemplation of one loving and it shapes it into certain experiences of spiritual or divine sweetness which it brings before the gaze of the spirit so that the spirit rejoices in them.
> And then, insofar as it is possible for man, worthy thoughts are entertained of God, if indeed the word "thought" *(cogitatio)* is correct where there is no impelling principle *(cogit)* nor anything impelled *(cogitur)*, but only awareness of God's abundant sweetness leading to exultation, jubilation and a true experience of the Lord in goodness on the part of the man who has sought him in this simplicity of heart.[20]

Let us round off this historical background with some passages from a younger contemporary of these Cistercian saints, Guigo II, Prior of the Grande Chartreuse. In his Monastic Ladder[21] he describes the four steps of *lectio divina:*

> One day while at manual labor, I began to think of one's spiritual exercise. At once four steps in the spiritual life came to mind: namely, reading *(lectio)*, meditation *(meditatio)*, prayer *(oratio)*, and contemplation *(contemplatio)*. These are the steps of the monastic ladder by which one rises from earth to heaven—few steps, indeed, but each of far-reaching and very great importance. This ladder, while

resting on the earth, penetrates the clouds and reaches into the secrets of heaven.[22]

In this pasage Guigo shows himself to be right in the heart of the centuries-long tradition of *lectio divina*. And he affirms the way of light—this ladder "penetrates the clouds and reaches into the secrets of heaven."

He goes on to delineate the functioning of each step:

> Reading is a search for the sweetness of the blessed life; meditation finds something of it; prayer begs for it; contemplation relishes what is obtained. . . . Seek by reading, and you shall find by meditation; knock by praying, and it shall be opened to you for contemplation. Reading, as it were, comes to the mouth as solid food; meditation bites it and masticates it; prayer acquires a taste for what is taken in; contemplation is the sweetness itself which delights and refreshes.[23]

He refines this further in a later summary:

> Spiritual reading takes first place, as it were, the foundation; and after it has set forth its material, it sends us onto meditation. Meditation then more earnestly inquires as regards the object sought; after digging, it finds the treasure and shows it. But when of itself it cannot obtain the treasure sought, meditation leads us on to prayer. Prayer, raising itself to God with all its strength, begs for the desired treasure, the sweetness of contemplation. When contemplation is arrived at, it repays the labor of the other three, while it refreshes the thirsting soul with the dew of heavenly refreshment. Reading, thèrefore, is a kind of exterior exercise; meditation, interior knowledge; prayer, a desire; but contemplation is above all perception.[24]

Guigo is decidedly opposed to gobbling up book after book without giving them a chance to do things to us. "Of what use is it to spend time in constant reading or to read hurriedly through the writings and lives of the saints, unless we extract the juice by chewing and ruminating the meat of what we read?" We need to "consider how we can act as they whose deeds we like to read about."[25]

Having pointed out that reading alone is not a sufficient response to the call and invitation of the Word, Guigo goes on to say how the steps are related and interdependent, as well as the defect or danger involved in isolating them:

> We can gather that reading without meditation is dry; meditation without reading is apt to err; prayer without meditation is not fervent; meditation without prayer is ineffectual; prayer with fervor seeks after contemplation; the attainment of contemplation without prayer is rare, or even miraculous.[26]

Making use of the Gospel incident at Jacob's well, Guigo gives us a life example of the interaction of Christ's invitation and the step-wise response of the Samaritan woman:

> [God] does work within us, but not altogether without our cooperation. . . . For indeed God wills that we help him; and, when he comes and awaits at the door, he wills that we open the affection of our will and lovingly acknowledge him. This acknowledgment he sought from the Samaritan woman when he said: "Call thy husband." As if he would say: "I wish to pour grace into your soul; make use of your free will." He was demanding a prayer from her when he said: "If you knew the gift of God, and who it is who says to you: Give me to drink; perhaps you would ask him for the living water." When she had heard this, the woman, instructed by reading, as it were, meditated in her heart that it would be good and useful for her to have this water. Enkindled, therefore, with the desire to possess, she turns to prayer, saying: "Lord, give me this water, that I may thirst no more, nor come here to draw water" (Jn. 4:16,10,15). She is roused to prayer. See how the hearing of the Lord's word, and the meditation following upon it, rouse her to prayer. For, how would she be anxious to ask, unless meditation had first enkindled her? Or what would the preceding meditation mean to her, unless the prayer following it begged for those things which meditation showed her should be asked for? Therefore, that meditation be fruitful, devout prayer should follow it; and the effect of that is the sweetness of contemplation.[27]

Prior Guigo proceeds to announce a monastic beatitude relating to the ladder of *lectio divina*:

> Happy is the man whose mind, freed from all other interest, habitually desires to occupy himself with these four steps: who, having sold all that he had, buys that field wherein is hidden the coveted treasure, namely, to be at leisure and to see how sweet is the Lord. Happy indeed, he who, when he has taken the first step, has practiced the second with care; has been devout in the third; and in the fourth, elevated above himself. For, by means of these ascents, which he has arranged in his heart, he will ascend from virtue to virtue, until he sees on Sion the God of gods.[28]

And thus, in effect, he—the man of prayer—will experience the fulfillment of the promise of Jesus, "I will love him and show myself to him."[29]

At this point, Guigo realizes that no one—our earthly situation being what it is—will remain for long in a state of being "lifted up to heaven" and he offers the obvious (?) practical solution of what to do after such exaltation:

> Since the vision of the human eye is weak and cannot bear for long the brightness of the true light, let him descend easily and in an orderly way to some one of the three steps by which he has ascended; and alternately, now on one, now on the other he delays as his will guides him, dictated by the place and time; aware now that he is the closer to God as he is further advanced from the first step.[30]

So much for historical background. It is now time to work together what we have witnessed into a way of practical procedures. These procedures will be given in terms of written texts and will not include that analogous realm of *lectio divina*, which pertains to listening to the book of nature, mentioned in the beginning of this chapter.

Practical Procedure for The Way of Lectio Divina

1. *Choose a quiet place*, a place where you can go every day as a habit, to read. *Take along the Holy Scriptures.* Choose the most appealing part of the New Testament or Old Testament for you, at least in the beginning weeks.

2. *Sit in a relaxed and restful position*, (or stand at some kind of a podium or lectern if you like). *Keep a pad or notebook or journal handy.* If you find that you are inclined to write a lot, you may prefer to sit at a table or desk.

3. As you are ready to begin, if you are enjoying inner peace, all is well. If you are agitated or restless, the first minutes of reading may quiet you, or they may not. It is safer to *start with a breathing and relaxing exercise.* The use of the Holy Name of Jesus for two or three minutes with the breathing exercise described in the previous chapter is an excellent preparation for *lectio divina.*

4. When you feel somewhat quieted, centered and ready to be alert to the text, *begin to read your chosen passage.* If you have previously read these paragraphs many times, you already know the gist of them. Consequently, you can now take them slowly, sentence by sentence, word by word. But if the passage is new for you, you may like to scan it momentarily to get some notion of where the passage is "going." Then come back and bite it off bit by bit.

5. If you feel inclined to read the words aloud, do so; or to mouth the words inaudibly and to stress and to draw out those words and phrases most richly laden with significance, do so. *Do whatever helps most to engage you with the text* and make it most meaningful for you. (It may take you ten years to complete the Bible this way, but that's all right, you are not going anywhere anyway except to heaven!)

6. *Keep in the periphery of your mind your one great solemn intention*, namely, to attempt or to desire to meet God through the text. Do not try to cover a chapter or a page or any predecided quantity. You want quality of experience, not quantity. Haste is the hatchet of destruction for this method of prayer.

7. Suppose our selected text for reading is the beginning of the Epistle to the Ephesians. We are *reading slowly* along. We may *pause over a sentence* or a clause, repeat it once, twice—*taste it fully*—and move on. We try to stay alert and catch the significance of every phrase and word. We may *repeat* a phrase and we may spontaneously *interpolate a phrase or word of our own*—which at the moment is a meaningful gloss or commentary for ourselves. When we find ourselves repeating, savoring, and interpolating, we are moving or escalating from *lectio* to *meditatio*. And the latter may lead us into *oratio*.

8. Let us take a concrete example of repeating, savoring and interpolating. Verse nine: "He has let us know [He has revealed] the mystery of his purpose [the mystery of his love; his purpose is sheer love!]." And we read on. We come to verse eleven: "...we were claimed as God's own [made God's very own!]." That does it! Something happens inside me. I am pervaded with a sense of God's goodness and love. Out of me leaps words of wonder and joy: "I am his! I belong to you! You love the likes of me? My God! it's too much! too much! I don't know what to do with myself! Let's read that again. Yes, You claimed me for your own. My Lord and my God. It says so. You are telling me. O Lord!" Depending on the gift of grace, the intensity of grace and my excitability,[31] I may soon be returning to slow reading, or I may be finished with the book for the next ten, twenty minutes or an hour. The book is forgotten and I am caught up in God's love. Nothing can substitute for him. I need nothing else for that period of prayer.

9. *When oratio spontaneously ceases, quietly and restfully go back to reading the text*—again repeating words and phrases, spontaneously interpolating, and staying open for the fountain of *oratio* to overflow as before. This practice can easily engage us without fatigue for an hour or two if we have the time available.

10. A *closing spontaneous prayer* of gratitude for the gift of the Scriptures and God's gift of himself to us is a fine way to terminate the period. Or we may prefer no closing prayer, as if to say, "Let my prayer of life continue now in another form." And we go off, carrying the mindfulness of God and his love in

our hearts, and even in the periphery of our minds as we live the other hours of our day.

Finally, keep a record in a notebook or journal of passages that touched you, adding a key word or two to indicate the content or significance for you.

Elaborations on the Practical Procedure

1. How important is it to have a quiet place to read and to be alone? Only your own experience can answer that. If "any old place" satisfies you, great. I have done *lectio divina* in a Greyhound bus terminal, the dentist and doctor's waiting rooms, and such like, but that was by force of the circumstances. I much prefer being alone and in a silent atmosphere. (For one thing, I am more free to speak the text aloud without disturbing others.) Most people would probably find in themselves this same preference.

I find it interesting that I am greatly tormented if someone runs a power mower outside my window when I am trying to prepare a class presentation, or a homily, or a community conference; whereas the same noise while I am doing *lectio divina* is no problem. This difference in reaction to the two situations helps me to see a difference in the nature of the situations. The first instance demands a lot of ego activity and psychic energy; it demands logical thinking, analysis, judgments and decisions. In the second instance I am letting go of ego control, being receptive, surrendering completely to God and what he is doing, as well as to all of the conditions of my surroundings. I can love and be at peace.

Another point worth keeping in mind about the selection of a place: God is everywhere; there is no necessity to go to read in a church or chapel and the like—unless, of course, we find this more conducive to prayer. The Kingdom of God is within; we bear him wherever we go. We are his holy place. We need only be at home with ourselves to be at home with him, and be at home for him. Sitting on a creek bank or on a park bench may be a help (so long as the mosquitos don't launch a stinging attack and draw us out of ourselves as they draw out our blood).

And what about using other books besides the Bible, such as theology, philosophy, life of a saint, religious psychology, even a novel? Several things must be considered. Obviously the Scriptures take pre-eminence bcause these writings are God's own self-revelation, written under the inspiration of the Holy Spirit, and the reader will enjoy the same Spirit's assistance in responding to them and to God's love revealed in them. Other writings can be of service. The guiding principle will always be "your one great solemn intention" (in procedure point six), namely, desiring sincerely to meet God in prayer through this text. But we must beware of slipping into an attitude of study, or using this particular book to help prepare for something else (an ulterior motive), or to satisfy curiosity, or because it is "more entertaining" and other such reasons. We should also remember that some reading content is more conducive to leading into *oratio* than other kinds.

Above all, we must be honest with ourselves and ask, "Do I really want to do *lectio divina now* or not? And do I want to do real *lectio divina*, or do I want to study or read for entertainment?" We have a need, and a legitimate need, for each of these areas as normal human beings. But it is good to be clear about what we are doing.

2. What should we do if we get sleepy during our *lectio divina*? We might try the solution of the monk quoted in the previous chapter where he says, "I lie down on the floor on my back, completely stretched out. I let my limbs and members go limp, and stay in this position for a minute or two. From actual experience I have found out that this short 'giving in' has the actual effect of a longer nap."[32] Other possibilities: standing and doing a physical exercise for a minute such as bending and touching toes, which brings blood to the brain (I had to do this one myself this morning!); making prostrations (as Orthodox monks do); taking a short jog; drinking a cup of tea or coffee if it is handy; or take a nap and re-scheduling the reading for a more alert time. But just to sit there and fight off sleep will leave us feeling dissatisfied with our prayer and will leave us without even the satisfaction of a sound snooze.

The great Elder Paisius Velichkovsky used to advise his monks: "So as to better bind one's attention to the content of the book being read, it is essential to follow the text word for word, and this is best done by copying out the book."[33] He acknowledged that this would not always be possible or appropriate, in which case it would be sufficient to copy out only the most important passages.

If writing during the reading helps attention and engagement with the text, do it. But we have to be on our guard that it does not take over and does not become "a new kind of thing" so that in fact we are taking notes *for some other purpose.*

3. What do we do if we are still feeling unsettled and unquieted within, even after two or three minutes using the Jesus Prayer? This sitution may require some ingenuity and spontaneity on our part, even to the extent, for example, of getting up and wheeling about in a kind of spontaneous ballet dance for a minute or so, and humming what is in your heart. This will help to relieve some of the physical and psychic tension that is causing the disquiet, and it may also inject a little humor and a refreshing sense of playfulness and freedom which won't hurt the situation at all. At some point, stop in your tracks as before the smiling face of the Lord. Then sit down and breathe his Holy Name as at the beginning, and try to read.

In the other direction—that of tranquility—it can sometimes happen when we start the Jesus Prayer that we feel drawn into *oratio* or true *contemplatio.* That is an attraction to be followed without restraint, and not only not regretfully, but gladly. To bypass the reading and go straight into prayer is fine. If we realize later that we are drifting into aimless thoughts and daydreaming, we should come back to the text, or the Jesus Prayer.

4. Scanning ahead on a fresh text is merely personal preference There is much to be commended in not looking ahead to see where the passage is going and just surrender to God.

5. It is common knowledge among monks that in the Middle Ages and in the long tradition of *lectio divina* "the reader usually pronounced the words with his lips, at least in a low tone and consequently, he hears the sentence seen by the eyes, just as today, in order to learn a language or a text, we

pronounce the words. This results in more than a visual memory of the written words. What results is a muscular memory of the words pronounced and an aural memory of the words heard."[34]

6. Yesterday I gave the pages which I had typed on the "Practical Procedures for the Way of *Lectio Divina*" to a confere and asked him to let me know if the steps seemed clear to him. He gave me a note this morning and among his comments was the following regarding step six: " 'One great solemn intention ... to meet God through the text'—this can't be emphasized enough. In going to *lectio*, I, in all my sinfulness and greatness, am going to meet my God in his holy word, during a holy time, in a holy place."

Lectio divina is a gift each time. "It is God who in his good will toward you, begets in you any measure of desire or achievement."[34a] It is God giving himself to me in some new way ... if I am "there" to meet him, and am open just for him. There must be at least a half-dozen passages in the Scriptures which refer to God as a jealous God—which means that we must be single-minded and single-hearted seekers and lovers at the time of prayer.

Hurried reading indicates that we have other motives and intentions lurking in our subconscious or unconscious. Just as there are alcoholics, sex-oholics, work-oholics, and perfect-oholics, we can become read-oholics and next-book-oholics. This speed is death to our serenity some of the time, and to our prayer most of the time.

The hired hand or employee *does* his work, in contrast with a child who "*be's*" his play. The hired hand does his work with a certain sense of necessity, and for reasons aside from the work itself. We need to become one with our reading the way the child becomes one with its play. We must go to our reading without hurry, with a sense of leisure, vacationing in God, if you like, (*vacatio Dei*).

7. "To meditate is to attach oneself closely to the sentence being recited and weigh all its words in order to sound the depths of their full meaning. It means assimilating the content of a text by means of a kind of mastication which releases its full flavor."[35] Dom Jean LeClercq, whom I have

just quoted, adds a quotation from the Cistercian, Arnoul of Boheriss: " 'When he reads, let him seek for savor, not science. The Holy Scripture is the well of Jacob from which the waters are drawn which will be poured out later in prayer....' "[36]

8. As the eyes, the lips and the mind read, the heart listens. Once the grace of the text, the word, the revelation touches the heart, it does its work. We respond, resonate with the exquisite love of God. He may touch us slowly, gradually, lightly, or violently. The faintest taste or fragrance of his presence sets us on the alert, alive to his love, and alive to whatever way he may manifest his intimacy. Blessed are those moments when he takes complete possession of us in his unforgetable embrace.

It is not sufficient for us to be told by someone that God is good and loves us. Being told does not yet give us a living realization of the fact. We need to experience his goodness. Only when he lays hold of us personally are we really ready to commit ourselves to him without reserve, without delay, without second thoughts.

9. There is nothing about this method of prayer that is physically or psychically draining, unless secondary motivation inserts itself. Only then does fatigue, weariness or restlessness set in. Otherwise this prayer can be sustained for quite long periods of time.[37]

To digress for a paragraph, I see this as good reason why this way of prayer would be helpful and consoling for retired people with a lot of time on their hands, ... not forgetting the senior citizen, the incapacitated, the chronically ill, shut-ins, anyone confined to home for any circumstance. All that is necessary is the desire for prayer, sufficient eyesight, and not to be so ill or weak as to make concentration difficult. Retired couples could help sustain each other by sharing the fruits of their *lectio divina* with each other. For example, they could each take something like an hour apart for *lectio* and then come together to talk about Holy Scripture and their experience of it and God. This could be very rewarding also for their mutual relationship.

While this way of prayer is suitable for long periods of time, it could also be helpful for something as short as ten or fifteen minutes, on the condition, of course, that we are already in a restful, receptive mood and don't have to take time quieting down. Should we happen to be enkindled by God's touch in that short time, and have to depart, we would feel a cleaving. On the other hand we would probably experience a spiritual and psychic boost as we tackle the next duty or service.

10. Along with many others, William of St. Thierry advised committing something to memory each day from our reading of Sacred Scripture.[38] This may be nothing more than an expression like "we were claimed as God's own." But a simple word such as this can be carried in our heart during the day and can have profound influence on the quality of our daily living. It can gently stir us to do everything for God. It can also have the effect of emptying our minds of inanities, of kindling expressions of love and trust in God, and bring back to us a sense of his loving and consoling presence—in a word, ongoing *meditatio* and *oratio*.

Opening prayers and closing prayers are verbalized expressions of our response to the grace of the present hour or event, expressions of thanksgiving, praise, adoration, contrition, love, and the like. The attitudes and dispositions expressed in these prayers can and hopefully do flow through the length and breadth of our day so that everything is united with the heart of the Father in Christlike living.

We will know that the good feelings, the joy, the love, the overflowing affections experienced often or seldom in our *lectio divina* are *authentic* if our life is becoming evermore Christlike. In other words, signs of true kindness, generosity and gentleness mark our relations with those around us, while our foolish attachments that make us avaricious, "cranky" and selfish are on the wane. If these good signs are not present, something is sick about our prayer and needs to be looked into and set right.

Finally, keeping a catalog or index of impressive passages of Holy Scripture, as well as of the other books we use for *lectio divina*, enables us at times of retreats and other special occasions to go back and re-experience something of those great moments of grace in our life. It becomes a record of goodness and gratitude, and therefore of love and joy.

So much for practical procedure.

Related Considerations

We look now at some related considerations about *lectio divina* to distinguish it from ordinary reading and study.

After completing the elaborations on the practical procedures, I had a dream the following night. I was praying and ministering in a church. When I came outside I met a young couple and asked them directions to some place where I had to go. They didn't seem to know the way. So I started down the road. I came to a little rise and a fork in the road. At the top of the rise I met a kindly old lady who seemed to live there at the fork on the rise. She directed me along the very branch which undoubtedly I would have taken if I hadn't met her. As I came down the mound there was a nice looking fellow standing beside a car. He asked if I were going to town and if I wanted a ride. Before I could answer, two of his cronies pushed me into the car and I found myself kidnapped as we sped toward the city.

Entering the city, he drove to his hideout and had to get me in without being seen, or at least without anything seeming to be wrong. The guy was rather fascinating in a way, and he was not mean or rough with me, nor did he tie me. All he wanted was that I cooperate in a scheme that he was planning. To get to the top of the hideaway he went first and one crony stayed behind me to prevent my escaping. We had to go up an almost vertical shaft and there were no stairs or elevator. He had a little motor attached to him by which he drew us all up behind him. As he neared the top of the shaft, he had to turn on a little kind of helicopter blade to lift us up over the lip of the shaft. I was fascinated by his ingenuity and had to smile. We sat down in a loft, far above the city.

I said I needed a shave but there was no electrical outlet up there. He gave me an interesting gadget to do the job. It had an electrode which I applied to one cheek and that supplied the current for running the "shaver." It didn't work too well and I said to myself, "I'm going to give this guy the slip, the first chance I get." At this point my alarm clock went off. I got up feeling all out of sorts.

Now what's the meaning of all that? My dreams over the

past few years have almost always been pleasant or at least neutral, and my feeling span upon awaking has been great, good or neutral. There seems to be a conflict in this case, with negative feelings.

In dream theory, all of the persons in the dream are aspects of myself. The four aspects present here are:

1. The "I" who is a pray-er and minister in church (and in fact I am a monk and priest).
2. The young couple.
3. The kindly, elderly lady.
4. The fascinating guy and his two cronies.

I notice that I am identifying with the one who prays and ministers. The young couple are nice but no help. I like the kindly old lady. And I don't really dislike the fascinating guy with all of his ingenuity, plans and inventions, nevertheless he is manipulating me, and I surely don't like that.

Probably the pray-er and the old lady image the contemplative and *anima* side of me, while the great fascinator is the activist and *animus* in me. And I don't know what to make of the young couple. But it looks like the activist, the controller in me is intruding on the contemplative and I'm not liking it at all.

It occurred to me that ever since I wrote Chapter Nine on the Jesus Prayer and Hesychasm, I have been feeling an attraction toward providing a richer place in my life for contemplative prayer. And yet, yesterday afternoon, "out of the blue" came a great storm of ideas for a new plot-plan for the garden, and almost immediately I was musing over several books I have had to put off reading until I finish my own. Plans, plans, plans! Then in comes Father Anthony to pick up this final chapter, as far along as I am on it, to give me a critique. His parting shot was, "I suppose you are already planning your next book." "Oh no, I'm not," I answered, "and there won't be any more!" Thereupon I found myself addressing those other bright ideas, "And as for the rest of you wise guys, *forget it!*"

So here we are, ready to scrutinize *lectio*. And before we are finished, this dream may be put to work in these closing pages.

Picture for a moment an intelligent college student who

has an engrossing interest in the great spiritual writers of the Christian past. He promises himself that as soon as he has completed his class assignments, he will settle down for the remainder of the evening and indulge his religious curiosity with one of his newly discovered treasures. And so he does. He settles in a plush chair, puffing on his pipe and sipping Old Crow as he speeds through the Dark Night. Next evening, the setting is the same, but now he is flying through The Cloud of Unknowing.

There are several commendable features about this scene. Having an interest in the great spiritual masters is marvelous. Relaxing in a comfortable chair and losing the day's tensions amid a little smoke and spirits is good for the psyche. And speed reading is not a skill to be sneezed at. It is certainly an asset for coping with any higher-gear college course.

However, the drawback in applying these attributes to the prayer process of *lectio divina* needs to be examined. Prayer, for the follower of Christ who invites us to struggle with the cross and die as the grain of wheat, begs for a different atmosphere, at least during the time of communing with the Lord.

Secondly, speed reading disrupts the process, for it not only wipes out miles of words in a hurry, but it also leaves the would-be inspirations of the Divine Word ungerminated in the dust of turning pages. When something has a hint of the precious about it, it is only natural to stop and linger upon it with the hidden hope that it will relinquish some of its mystery to us and stir our soul to a greater level of life. Whether a breath-taking sight, an exquisite fragrance, or harmonious sound—all invite us to savor them, and reap their blessing. It is not different with spiritual realities and Divine invitations.

Thirdly, an attitude of filial reverence is asked for in *lectio divina*. This respectful attitude, which includes a serious caring and gentle receptivity, avoids treating God and the spiritual life as an object of curiosity, even though pious curiosity.

There are choice sections in the writings of the Fathers, the saints and the mystics (to say nothing of Sacred Scripture) which reached the page through the revealing help of God, and they give up their secret only to careful, reverent searching— namely, when the reader is as disposed to receive them as the author was before him.

The nature of *lectio divina* becomes clearer when we compare it with "study," which is the process of acquiring facts and knowledge.

Study:

—is an I-it relationship

—may be purely intellectual, "cerebral," gratifying only a part of our self and unrelated to the rest of life

—may be merely an accumulation of facts; but it may also be a deep search for meaning, oriented toward the up-building of life and its integration

—involves analysis and distinction; it may or may not lead to synthesis

—is a "heady," masculine type of activity
—works the text over and pursues it
—is a process of critical, systematic inquiry and theorizing; demands verification and judgment regarding truth

Lectio divina:

—is an I-Thou relationship ... communicating with a friend who is *present.*

—is prayer, engaging affectivity as well as intellect; it touches the whole person and relates to our deeper needs and to every aspect of life.

—is contact with the Word hidden in the word and standing behind the word; it leads to reconciliation, forgiveness, healing; it is therapeutic, integrating, and sanctifying—thus establishing us in peace

—it merges us, bonds us with God, helps us to become one will and one spirit with him

—is a more intuitive, feminine type of activity
—listens and waits on the Lord to give
—is non-critical and a cultivation of receptivity and docility, of openness and surrender to Truth and Love revealing and offering himself[39]

In actual life we need both study and prayer, regardless of our profession in life, not excluding the monastic way of life. It is a matter of striking a balance; a balance that is suitable to our vocation, and our personal call from the Lord. The ideal of course would be to reach such a synthesis within ourselves that we are always occupied with a "restful search for God on the two levels: thought and person."[40] This means that we learn gradually to make God the center, the focus, the intent of all that we do . . . in a gentle and loving way. This becomes a deep-seated disposition and it is continual prayer.

This is a happy state to be in. To come to it, however, certain things must feed into it and nourish it along. And we must be willing to pass through periods of confusion and disorientation; in other words, there must be moments when we feel that we are disintegrating before we discover that in fact we are experiencing stages of integration.

In this age of literacy and sophistication, it would be a rare person who would not find some study of Scriptural exegesis, history, philosophy, theology (both moral and dogmatic) and psychology helpful in his or her ongoing conversion. Studies in reasonable amount and with a God-centered frame of mind are a stabilizing factor in our growth. They help us to situate ourselves in the realities of life and to grow beyond that weird world of our own naive fantasy-making, full of sentimentalities and rash cogitations. They help to put us in touch with the realities of salvation history (beyond our own little horizon) and the penetrating depths and demands of the ascetical and mystical life. Such nourishment will help to make our prayer authentic.

While moderate studies in the beginning are helping to stabilize our prayer, the quiet time of prayer itself is a "natural" time for our memory to cough up incidents of an incredible array. There will be pleasant events and persons of the past and the present. There will be devastating surges of painful and pressing difficulties, old wounds and new, with their accompanying feelings and strong emotions. Ill-fated interpersonal encounters will spill out into our consciousness all of our apprehensions and suspicions, our anxieties, antagonism and

hatreds, our selfishness and self-centeredness, our self-con-
sciousness and self-pity, our anger and arrogance. Everything
comes up.

But it couldn't be at a better time. Why? Because it is a
time when we are more likely to face up to our little inner Job's
heap in the presence of the Lord and experience his compassionate and healing help.

Nevertheless, if our prayer is so to say, "out of our own
head," of our "own making," during the time of these surges
and storms, we will experience them rather intensely. On the
other hand, if we are engaged in the process of *lectio divina*, the
contact with the word of Scripture will soften the pounding of
the waves. This word of revelation, backed by the living Word
will be an assurance and support to stand upon or abide in
while these salty waters flow away leaving us cleansed and not
battered and rusted out.

In fact, the word of Scripture itself confronts us with our
faults and sins and helps to cleanse us. The word instructs us in
true repentance. We learn to "own" our selfish attachments as
our own and to lay them before the Lord. We humbly submit
to Him. "Here I am, Lord. This is the way I am. I need your
saving help. In your love help me."

Lectio divina is creative in what it brings alive in us; it is
redemptive in what it rectifies in us; and it is sanctifying in the
person we meet, and share our life with, and are given a share
in his life. The word instructs us in the mind and outlook of
Christ, while Christ himself imbues us with his outlook and
transforms us so that we become gentle, peaceful and compassionate like unto him. Thus, apparent disintegration serves—is
at the service of—our integration of personality in the personality of Christ.

Meditatio

While reading (*lectio*) puts us in contact with the word,
meditatio is the attempt to make the word and the depths of its
meaning completely our own. This engagement with the word
of the text is expressed by terms like: pondering, weighing,
reflecting, considering, mulling, chewing, ruminating, won-

dering, cherishing, savoring; relating, associating, recalling, remembering, memorizing, and others.

At the touch of grace our engagement with the word deepens. We become more alive and engrossed. The word lays hold of us, grips us, excites us, draws us in. We experience Christ's experience along with him (in the case of reading the Gospels), we find ourselves taking sides, we are shaped interiorly. We develop attitudes and convictions. We realize ever more fully what the Lord is offering us and asking of us (for our own benefit and happiness). As we ponder, the Word reveals himself to us; and as he does so, he reveals us to ourselves in our relationship with him. We come to know both him and ourselves, and our greatness because of him.

Meditatio thus makes the word a living part of ourselves; thereafter it is ours to use to give expression to our dialogue with God.

Oratio

As *lectio* puts us in contact with the word of the text and *meditatio* enables us to tap into richer meanings beyond the word, we can say that *oratio* puts us in contact with the Word behind the word, in personal dialogue.

An example of this movement to *oratio* from *lectio* and *meditatio* happened to me at Vespers this evening. After the choral psalmody, the monks sat down and the reader took up his book and began the scheduled reading for the "Saturday of the Fifth Week of Easter," taken from one of St. Augustine's discourses on the psalms.[41] "The season before Easter signifies the troubles in which we live here and now, while the time after Easter which we are celebrating at present signifies the happiness that will be ours in the future. What we commemorate before Easter is what we experience in this life; what we celebrate after Easter points to something we do not yet possess. This is why we keep the first season with fasting and prayer; *but now the fast is over....*" That is as much as I heard. At the words "now the fast is over" by spontaneous association the words from the Song of Songs sprang from my memory, "and the winter is over and gone, come my beloved, come!" A prayer of desire and gratitude flamed out and filled the minutes of silence after the reader sat down.

A few minutes later the cantor intoned the Hymn of Mary (the *Magnificat*) and her words "the Almighty has done great things for me; holy is his Name" became my own to voice my thanksgiving for the preceding moments of happy prayer.

Several comments on this experience: the movement from *lectio* to the association of words (*meditatio*) and the leap into direct address and communing (*oratio*) was rapid and spontaneous. Furthermore, my memory did not serve up for me the exact quotation,[42] but that is unimportant. The main thing is that it evoked a personal communing with God.

Dom Jean LeClercq explains the phenomenon as follows:

> This way of uniting reading, meditation and prayer, this "meditative prayer" as William of St. Thierry calls it, had great influence on religious psychology. It occupies and engages the whole person in whom the Scripture takes root, later to bear fruit. It is this deep impregnation with the words of Scripture that explains the extremely important phenomenon of reminiscence whereby the verbal echoes so excite the memory that a mere allusion will spontaneously evoke whole quotations and, in turn, a scriptural phrase will suggest quite naturally allusions elsewhere in the sacred books. Each word is like a hook, so to speak; it catches hold of one or several others which become linked together . . .[43]

If *meditatio* has the power to benefit our psychic and moral life, *oratio* does so even more richly. The ardent dynamism of *oratio* draws us toward a deeper interiority and inner directedness. It reaches beyond the printed word to touch the other who gives meaning to all else. In that communion he shares his meaning of life, created and uncreated.

As the intimacy of *oratio* deepens, everything begins to be seen as gift. All is received from God. And God himself gives himself as Infinite Gift. Nothing evokes *oratio* more frequently nor ardently after that than gratitude. And gratitude continues to hollow out the heart to receive him more and more, until death consummates the hollowing out and makes possible complete union and total giving.

Tears, both outward and inward (i.e., the inward weeping of the heart), are a frequent companion of gratitude. Such tears are part of an ardor where gratitude is accompanied by compunction, a sense of undeservedness, and the like. They both deepen and sustain the prayer, and at the same time maintain a sense of peace and gentleness of heart. When gratitude wells up from awareness of the utter goodness of God without any self-inclusion, its fruit is sheer joy in his existence, without tears.

When we go to work, reading stays behind, but not *meditatio* and *oratio*. The word of *lectio divina* and choral office which we have made our own comes with us as a food to nourish us. We reminisce on it, associations occur to us, and it continues to grow in meaning within us through the persons we meet and live with, and through the events of the day. In pleasant and difficult moments, prayer springs from our hearts in the language of the word that is rooted in us. It is *meditatio* and *oratio* which imbue work with a proper orientation and sense of dedication to the two-fold commandment of love.

In monasticism, *lectio divina* and the choral office are seen as two expressions of prayer, which are closely related. They are composed of the same principal elements and only the execution of them differs. One is private and individualistic and the other is public and communal. In *lectio divina*, the reading is to oneself and one listens in solitude, meditates as one chooses on a text personally chosen, with less limitations on prayer and contemplation. At the choral offices, all chant the text of the psalms and a reader reads a selected prose passage for all to listen to. Obviously there must be limitations on the external expression of each participant's *meditatio* and *oratio*. (And if one gets sleepy, he can't very well jump up and do a ballet.) Whereas if anyone experiences *contemplatio*, there is no problem, for the others continue right on with the text of the office.

Contemplatio

A final time we can say, *lectio* puts us in contact with the word and *meditatio* brings us to the richer meanings hidden behind the word; and then as *oratio* puts us in contact with Christ, the Word behind the word, in personal dialogue, *contemplatio* carries us into the indescribable depths of God hidden in Christ, Who takes us to the Father in Love.

"Carries us into" picturesquely connotes movement from place to place. This is initially helpful to come to grips with the glorious reality of *contemplatio*. But we must eventually see it in a totally transcendent way.

"Carries us into" also tells us that something is happening to us, that something is being done for us, that we are not expending a lot of physical or psychic energy, that we are in a condition of restfulness and repose. It hints that someone else is present with us; and in the context of *contemplatio*, he is active, we are receptive. He is giving, we are receiving; he is giving something of himself and we are receiving him. Gift. Exquisite gift . . . with his peace, love and joy. And eventually, bridal gift, with indestructible peace and ecstatic love and joy. A bridal gift that is union. Consummate union. Two become one. *Unitas Spiritus.*

In the imagery of Sacred Scripture, the bride has become a princess, a queen for the king of kings. She strolls with her Lover; she dances before him, she dances with him. She is beautiful with his beauty, lovely as the rainbow. But she is not focused on what he has done for her, so much as engaged with who he is, who has become all the treasure of her heart. She entertains him, amuses him, plays with him as Rebecca with Isaac, making love together as bride and king.

This symbolism points to the human person's complete acceptability to the Lord of creation, redemption and sanctification. It points to the total response of person to person, a rich sense of complete belonging, mutual possession, presence with, of intimate friendship, companionship, fellowship, of joyful, loving union that spells bliss for the recipient of consuming love.

But these are just words, words, words! They are doomed to failure. There is no way to capture the reality in words. Each person in prayer must experience it for himself or herself. If meeting the Mother of God in prayer is enough to pluck one's heart strings and "tear them in ribbons,"—and she is only human like ourselves—what hope is there to convey the experience of meeting the Lord, as human and Divine? To say nothing of the Father and the Holy Spirit!

I am letting enthusiasm carry me away. We must go back to the beginning.

The experience of *contemplatio* will be somewhat rare for the beginner in prayer, and it may not be a very deep or intense one from the aspect of experiencing the presence of God. This will be especially true in the case of that *contemplatio* which we considered in Chapter Five under the term of "prayer of simple gaze." Likewise infused *contemplatio*, as mentioned at the beginning of Chapter Seven will be an isolated event, although in such instances the experience, though infrequent, can be intense. (One of the big dangers for beginners, whether after their conversion or a re-conversion, is the illusion that their many sensible consolations are infused prayer.)

After some years or perhaps only months of the practice of *lectio divina*, *contemplatio* in the sense of prayer of simple gaze can be quite frequent, depending upon our willingness to surrender, or let go of, our drive to keep our prayer active. But as far as infused contemplation is concerned, we cannot know the day or the hour; we can only dispose ourselves in faithful love and leave it to the Lord to provide as he sees fit for our welfare, which he has very much at heart. Knowing God's great love, we might well wonder why infused prayer is not much more common. We must admit that the obstacles arise and are clung to by ourselves; on God's side there is only sheer generosity.

It is far, far from exaggeration to claim that the most exquisite joy and peace which a human person can have in this life will be experienced as prayer directly relating to intimate communion with the God of love. I am not saying that such experience will come early in life ... perhaps only toward the end of a long and faithful giving of self to God in prayer.

For the remainder of this section on *contemplatio*, we are concerned with infused prayer. When God's blessed day and hour have arrived for us, our spiritual journey becomes an excursion into joy and the deepening of every virtue in ways we never suspected possible. Let us begin with an observation by St. Bernard:

There is another form of divine contemplation, very different from the former because it takes place in the interior, when God himself is pleased to visit the soul that seeks him, provided it is committed to seeking him with all its desire and love. We are told what the sign of such a visit is by one who experienced it. "Fire goes before him and burns up his adversaries round about." The fire of holy desire ought to precede his advent to every soul whom he will visit, to burn up the rust of bad habits and so prepare a place for the Lord. The soul will know that the Lord is near when it perceives itself to be aflame with that fire, and can say as the Prophet did: "He has sent a fire from on high down into my bones, and enlightened me;" and again: "My heart became hot within me and in my meditation fire burst forth."[44]

From this passage we see how important a place desire and longing for God has in the experience of infused prayer. The strong habit of desire and love dispose us for it; and the kindled act of that love is the immediate foretaste of his visit.

In another passage St. Bernard shares something of his own infused experience:

The Word is living and effective, and as soon as ever he has entered into me, he has aroused my sleeping soul, and stirred and softened and pricked my heart, that hitherto was sick and hard as stone. . . . I knew that he was present only by the movement of my heart; I perceived his power because it put my sins to flight and exercised a strong control on all my impulses. I have been moved to wonder at his wisdom too, uncovering my secret faults and teaching me to see their sinfulness; and I have experienced his gentleness and kindness . . .; and, in the renewal and remaking of . . . my inmost being, I have beheld to some degree the beauty of his glory and have been filled with awe as I gazed at his manifold greatness.[45]

An altered state of consciousness is clearly expressed where St. Bernard says that his sleeping soul, sick and hard as stone came alive with a movement of the heart. He goes on to point out how he experienced a renewal and remaking of his spirit, of his inmost being. In contrast with the awareness of his own sinfulness and hidden faults revealed to him, he experiences something of the power and the wisdom of the Lord, of his gentleness and kindness, and something of the beauty of his glory and manifold greatness. In other words this experience can be summarized as a personal moral uplifting and an enjoyed sense of God's presence in his goodness and loveliness. All infused prayer effects moral betterment in the recipient's life by way of an increase of virtue and the dispositions of the Holy Spirit, and certainly a deeper attachment to God's will and a stronger inclination to a life of prayer. This does not mean that the person is immediately conscious of this increase. The sense of God's presence (or his conspicuous absence in some cases) is the heart of the experience, and is often accompanied by a strong affective response to his presence, with no little joy. Furthermore, the receiver, with no effort on his or her part, is frequently enriched with a galaxy of impressions and intuitive lights about God himself and his divine plan for creation. These become the food for future meditation and prayer of gratitude, and keep disposing the heart for future infusions of prayer.

These facts are manifested in the Cistercian abbot Baldwin of Ford as recounted by Dom Jean LeClercq:

> Baldwin of Ford often describes his attitude in the presence of the Eucharist by these two words: *stupor et admiratio*. He is surprised, rapt, as in an ecstasy, in a state which partakes both of the immobility caused by astonishment and the spontaneous elan provoked by enthusiasm; he never grows accustomed to the sublime realities on which his glance lingers; his wonder never diminishes; he marvels at the mystery revelation proposes for contemplation, and he also marvels at the fact that men believe in it in the Church: he marvels at the faith. His admiration rewards and, at the same time, stimulates his faith, and these two dispositions of the soul augment each other mutually. They awaken the intelligence and all the other faculties of man; reflection and understanding are benefited by admiration and, in turn foster charity and all the other virtues, and mystical experience and asceticism flow from them.[46]

This passage contains more than a hint of the typically cataphatic mysticism of the Cistercians. This is the mysticism

of knowing rather than unknowing, of affirmation than nega-
tion, of inner faith/love experience of the God of revelation,
who "reaches down" to touch us where we are, in all our
littleness, weakness and need.

Contemplatio continually evolves in richness and intensity;
it introduces the heart and affections to all good; it broadens
the horizons of consciousness with divine realities, with exquisite insights into the mystery of God. All of this is the sheer gift
of one who loves. St. Bernard expresses this in the imagery of
Sacred Scripture, particularly the Song of Songs:

> For the various desires of the soul it is essential that the
> taste of God's presence be varied too, and that the infused
> flavor of divine delight should titillate in manifold ways the
> palate of the soul that seeks him.... He comes ... like a
> magnificent and powerful king, giving courage to his timid
> and poverty-stricken bride, stirring up her desire by show-
> ing her the ornaments of his glory, the riches of his wine-
> presses and storehouse, the produce of his gardens and
> fields, and finally introducing her into his private apart-
> ments. For "her husband's heart has confidence in her,"
> and among all his possessions there is nothing that he
> thinks should be hidden from her whom he redeemed from
> indigence, whose fidelity he has proved, whose
> attractiveness wins his embraces. And so he never ceases, in
> one way or another, to reveal himself to the inward eye of
> those who seek him, ...[47]

Depending upon the intensity and nature of our desire,
the termination of these periods of infused prayer may leave us
overflowing with gratitude and a return to *oratio* with an
affectionate outpouring of active prayer. On the other hand,
we may experience a great sense of emptiness and loss, and
continue languishing for a return of the Lord and the delightful sense of his presence and companionship. St. Bernard describes this experience in his own colorful way:

> When the Lord withdraws himself from me, it is as when a
> fire is taken from beneath a boiling pot; my fervor and
> devotion languish and grow cold, and that is how I know
> that he has gone. My soul is then inevitably sad, till he

return and my heart kindle in me once again. And, having
known the blessedness of his indwelling once, how can I do
otherwise than cry "Return.!" as does the bride? As long as
I live, that word of recall shall be mine. As often as he
leaves me, so often will I call him back, and I will pray him
to return, not empty-handed but "full of grace and truth,"
as he is wont to do, as he did yesterday, and the day
before.[48]

Note that Bernard is receiving infusions, not a few times a
year or several times a month, but on an habitual daily basis.
Here is how he expresses his waiting and yearning for the
return: " 'A little while and you shall not see me; and again a
little while and you shall see me!' O little while and little while,
O lengthy little while! Good Lord, do you call that a little
while in which we do not see you? With all good respect to
your word, my Lord, I must confess that it is long to me—yes,
much too long."[49]

The fruit of these visits is of undreamed of worth. God
becomes dear beyond description. He is Father and Mother.
He is Lord and Savior and Shepherd, High Priest and King,
Brother and Bosom Friend, Ecstatic Bridegroom. He is con-
stant Companion and Inner Life. God is vividly REAL at last.
He is love. He is sweetness. He is intimate mutual possession.
He is living joy. He is the Joy-Person behind all other reality.
Joy, Happiness, Bliss.

We learn that we are truly born of God, born of his love.
We learn what it means to be a kissed and caressed child, to be
a cherished son and daughter. We delight in our discipleship,
in our salvation, in the rich pastures of sanctification, in being
of the People of God, a kingly people and royal priesthood. We
rejoice in being a brother, a sister, a true friend, a chosen
spouse of Infinite Charm. We enjoy the intimate presence and
companionship of joy in person—Joy, Peace, Patience, Kindness, Goodness, Trustfulness, Gentleness and Self-Possession.
He is All and giving all, All, to us.

These visits are the gathering point of all our love. It is as
though all of our loves, the great ones and the little ones of our
life, are brought together, multiplied, and transcended. The
most endearing moments and deepest intimacy we have shared

with our father or mother, husband or wife, brother or sister, or dearest friend are united in a burst of love for God. We become a flame of love for God and God is Love's Flame for us.

The wonder of it all is that our earthly loves in these moments are enhanced, purified in the furnace of his love, and intensified for the sake of him. We are given, we are imbued with a deeper respect, compassion, empathy, charity, for all of our dear ones, all of our acquaintances, all whom we live with. (This is the sign, the test, that our prayer is authentic and not just a self-centered illusion and a sick ego-trip. Only by our fruits can we know.)

We feel an intimate part of our Father's creation; we expand with a sense of belonging; and we know that it is all a gift for us from him. Our lot is with angels and archangels and a whole host of heavenly persons. We gain a mother with whom we will be the bride of the heavenly Jerusalem. We gain innumerable brothers and sisters in those who have gone on before us. Their love becomes a conscious influence, their presence a communion and dialogue with the saints . . . for we are God's family.

Surely *contemplatio* is the ultimate in psychotherapy, a process of "sanctotherapy." And it's all gift. It is free, like the sunshine, and the rain. May we listen avidly to the heavenly bridegroom and the shepherd of our race calling out to us:

> Oh, come to the water all you who are thirsty;
> though you have no money, come!
> Buy corn without money, and eat,
> and, at no cost, wine and milk.
> Why spend money on what is not bread,
> your wages on what fails to satisfy?
> Listen, listen to me,
> and you will have good things to eat
> and rich food to enjoy.
> Pay attention, come to me;
> listen, and your soul will live.[50]

Remember my dream some pages back? In the week that has passed since that dream, one theme keeps coming to mind: Stop and listen to him! As an American, raised in a competitive, activist society, I am not at all likely to fall into Quietism. My great danger is to get in the Lord's way of doing for me what he wants to do by my neglecting—all too innocently—to be quiet enough interiorly to hear his whisper of love. To hear him I must quiet the inner noise and flurry. I'm moving too fast to pick up the free corn, wine and milk. And if I should manage to fetch a little on the fly, I'm in too much of a hurry to enjoy it. When I learn to listen, I will truly live life at a godly depth, in the realm of love where life is richest and most fulfilling.

There will always be more things available to do each day than I am able to do. And there is no end to it. The solution is to learn to let go of what is unnecessary. To be busy in unnecessary ways is easy; to discern and put aside or put off the unnecessary is not easy, but it is the key to success in prayer. The temptation to continue as I am is with me because I am sure to think that the little things I do are important and necessary. The truly necessary have a way of leaving me in inner peace. I am at peace within and without. But unnecessary things have a way of twisting me up inside, and it shows up outside. My unconscious seems to know the difference and lets me know via my feelings. And if I don't listen to my feelings, I may have a dream! "Listen, and your soul will live!"

All the Lord wants is to lead me to a communion of wills (*communio voluntatum*), an accord in love (*consensus in caritate*), a complete oneness with himself (*unitas spiritus*). His desire for me is the complete purity—godlikeness - of my heart (and this is sublimely more than mere freedom from lust). He wants to build in me such a purity of heart that I come to be moved by nothing but what draws me to him, nothing but what pleases his heart. My yes, my *fiat*, will be all yes and amen. All my psychic energy, all my affectivity will be invested in my return of God's love. Julian of Norwich has this touching thing to say of Christ's love for us: "He said full sweetly this word: 'If I might suffer more, I would suffer more.' He said not if it were needful to suffer more; but, 'If I might suffer more.' For though it were not needful, and he might suffer more, he would."[51]

Conclusion

Regarding the Three Techniques

If the reader feels that it would be a help to follow one of the three "techniques" presented in this book, how would he or she decide which one would be most suitable? (This could make another book.)

In general, our personal vocation and situation in life has much to do with our choice of ways of reaching out for God. Our prayer should be in balance with our life. It should help to shape our day and yet be contoured with our day. Otherwise, our prayer efforts will produce needless tension and add more disruption to our life. We may need a variety of ways to pray, active and receptive, to suit our changing circumstances.

For the monk and vowed religious, a balanced life will include Community Prayer, Eucharist and sacramental life, ongoing exposure to God's word, and private communing with God in one or more ways. The lay person's life should also have a balance of these elements, although the frequency will normally be less.

Now, what about these methods of prayer? My opinion is that anyone attempting Centering Prayer or the Jesus Prayer in a somewhat exclusive way for his or her private communing with God will be helped tremendously on the condition that he or she has spent sufficient time (perhaps several good years) in delving into the Sacred Scriptures and knowing Christ in his own word. But the condition mentioned is an important one,

150

and I base it on my experience in spiritual directing as well as on the view of the author of The Cloud of Unknowing. Read his Chapter 35. In part, he advises that: "Anyone who aspires to contemplation ought to cultivate *Study, Reflection,* and *Prayer,* or to put it differently, reading, thinking, and praying."[1] In other words he recommends the way of *lectio divina* until we have reached a certain maturity in the life of prayer. And that maturity is based on knowing the Scriptures. Even so, the Scriptures will continue to hold a balanced place in some form in real spiritual maturity. The author of The Cloud cautions: "Beginners and those little advanced who do not make the effort to ponder God's word should not be surprised if they are unable to pray. Experience bears this out." He says this a second time more intensely, "So I want you to understand clearly that for beginners and those a little advanced in contemplation *reading or hearing* the word of God must precede pondering it and without time given to *serious reflection* there will be *no genuine prayer.*"[2]

On the other hand, to spend a couple of short periods each day in Centering Prayer or the Jesus Prayer and to spend some time also in reading and meditating on Sacred Scripture each day would be a happy combination, even for novices toward the end of their novitiate.

To adopt and use the invocation and the tranquil attitude of Centering Prayer and the Jesus Prayer as we live through the events of our day is an admirable application of these methods to our daily life, and highly commendable.

The way of *lectio divina* has an advantage in being suitable for beginners, for "illuminates" and for the greatly advanced. The beginner has the word to work on and make his own. The more knowledgeable illuminate will move more rapidly from contact with the word to contact with God in *oratio.* And the greatly advanced will fly quickly into *contemplatio,* the mysticism of light. And so, *lectio divina* is a way that is suitable all through life.

Whatever ways we decide to pray, let the decisions be guided by the Holy Spirit who always breathes our prayer with us.

Notes

Introduction

1. I am indebted to Fr. Chrysogonus Waddell, OCSO, of Gethsemani Abbey, Kentucky, for this account of Brother Bruno. (Retreat Conference #4, November 1976, given at New Clairvaux.) Also see Psalm 100.3 (Hebrew enumeration).

2. John 1:9.

Chapter One

1. St. Bernard of Clairvaux, Sermon 83 #4 on the Song of Songs, in Terence L. Connoly, S.J., *Saint Bernard on the Love of God* (London: Burns, Oates and Washbourne Ltd., 1937), p. 230. (See also, below, the quotations of William of St. Thierry on being one will, one spirit, with God.)

2. John 1:3,4. (Scripture quotations are from *The Jerusalem Bible*, Garden City, Doubleday & Co., Inc., 1966, unless otherwise stated.)

3. Acts 17:28.

4. Psalm 33:9,5.

5. He is the great "A Se;" we, the little "ab Alio's"!

6. The Easter Proclamation (Exsultet).

7. II Corinthians 5:21—*The Living Bible*, (Wheaton: Tyndale House Pub., 1971).

8. Ephesians 1:3-14.

9. One of my 16 great, great grandparents was in the Civil War. He rceived a furlough and made his way back home. It was at the time of this unpredictable furlough that he sired my great grandfather. No furlough, no me. Or a single chunk of lead finding its mark before the furlough . . .!

9a. I suppose this example comes to mind because of an experience at work one day. A postulant and I were clearing away brush

along an irrigation slough (canal). We came upon a thick grape vine
dangling from high-up in a branch of a large oak. We each took a
couple of swings across the slough on the vine just as a couple of
small youngsters from nearby Vina passed along. Their eyes spoke
their wish, so I instructed one of them carefully how to hang on and
when to let go. He made a successful flight, and jumped for joy for
another try. The second lad lost his grip in mid-course and went
down with a splash. We helped him out of the knee-deep mud and
water, his seat plastered in brown and his cowboy boots
"squooshing" at every step. I never did hear what his mother had to
say!

10. I John 3:2.

11. Romans 6:5. ("made us vitally one" is *symphytoi* in the Greek).

12. Isaiah 5:4. I am indebted to Fr. Bernard Leeming, S.J., for
this engaging rendition of part of St. Bernard's sermon "On the
Three Degrees of Love"—from a taped conference given by Fr.
Leeming to the community of New Clairvaux during Holy Week,
1964.

13. I've read it and heard it preached that the sufferings and
death of Jesus are so efficacious for redemption (in the sense of
"buying back" from sin) that if there were other races on other
planets in need of redemption, these incarnate events would suffice
for all peoples and universes. I don't doubt the truth of this claim. But
realizing the love of God, neither do I doubt that if ever another
generation springs up on some stellar satellite who stand in need of
redemption, that the heavens will open and rain down the Just One
... giving them also the joy of seeing him among them, in their
likeness, a part of them, one with them, belonging to them, and they
to him.

14. The information of the last three paragraphs comes from
personal notes of many years ago; I no longer remember the original
sources of the notes.

15. The associated reference to the hazel nut came to me from a
beautiful passage of Julian of Norwich which bears quoting:

> "...He shewed a little thing, the quantitie of a hasel-nutt,
> lying in the palme of my hand, as me seemed; and it was as
> round as a ball. I looked thereon with the eie of my under-
> standing, and thought, 'What may this be?' and it was
> answered generallie thus: *It is all that is made.* I marvelled
> how it might last; for me thought it might sodenlie have
> fallen to naught for litleness. And I was answered in my

understanding, *It lasteth, and ever shall: for God loveth it. And so hath all thing being by the love of God.*

In this litle thing I sawe three properties. The first is, that God made it. The second is, that God loveth it. The third is, that God keepeth it. But, what beheld I therein? verilie the Maker, the Keeper, the Lover. For till I am substanciallie united to him, I maie never have full rest, ne verie blisse; that is to saie that I be so fastned to him, that there be right nought that is made betweene my God and mee. This litle thing that is made, me thought it might have fallen to nought for litleness. Of this needeth us to have knowledge, that us liketh naught all thing that is made, for to love God, have God that is unmade." From XVI Revelations of Divine Love Shewed to Mother Juliana of Norwich 1373, (London: Kegan, Paul, Trench, Trubner and Company, Ltd., 1902), pp. 12,13.

16. Wisdom 11:22.

Chapter Two

1. Here we get the fuller picture–in the light of the Paschal Mystery–of 1 Thessalonians 5:16-19 and Luke 18.1 which we will be examining in Chapter 3.
2. Acts Chapters 26, 22, 9.
3. Acts 26:16.
4. Acts 26:18.
5. Acts 26:19, 20.
6. Romans 8:13, 9; Galatians 3:2, 5; Ephesians 4:7, 8; I Corinthians 2:12; 6:11; 13: 4-7 and 13; 12:4-6; 12:7-11; Romans 12:6; and many other texts.
7. I Corinthians 12:27, 28; Romans 12:5; Ephesians 4:12; 5:22-32; Revelation 19:8; 21: 2, 9.
8. Ephesians 4:13.
9. Colossians 3:9, 10; Romans 6:6.
10. Galatians 3:27.
11. Galatians 2:19, 20; Romans 6:10,11.
12. II Corinthians 5:17; Ephesians 2:15.
13. Ephesians 2:10.
14. Ephesians 2:4-6.
15. Romans 8:15.

16. I Thessalonians 4:17, 18.
17. I Thessalonians 5:18.
18. John 14:15-17.
19. John 14:20, 23.
20. John 14:27.
21. John 14:27 in *The Living Bible*.
22. John 17:22-24.
23. John 15:11.
24. John 16:20-22.
25. John 17:21, 22.
26. John 17:23, 24.
27. I Corinthians 6:17.
28. William of St. Thierry was a pre-scholastic medieval theologian, mystic, intimate friend of St. Bernard, Benedictine abbot and later a Cistercian monk; died about 1148 before he completed the *Vita Prima*, the life of St. Bernard.
29. William of St. Thierry, *Exposition on the Sons of Songs*, Song One, Stanza Eight, #95; trans. Mother Columba Hart, O. S. B., *The Works of William of St. Thierry*, vol. 2, (Cistercian Fathers Series 6) p. 78.
30. William of St. Thierry, *The Golden Epistle: A Letter to the Brethren of Mont Dieu*, II:XV, 257, 258; trans. Theodore Berkeley, O.C.S.O., *The Works of William of St. Thierry*, vol. 4 (Cistercian Fathers Series 12) p. 94.
31. Ibid. II:XVI, 262, 263; pp. 95, 96.
32. John 14:21 (emphasis mine).
33. Psalm 34:8.
34. John 14:9.
35. The reference here is particularly to the priest-psychologist Adrian Van Kaam and to Father Louis Merton, O.C.S.O.
36. John 14:21.
37. Philippians 2:5-8.
38. John 6:51 and 56.
39. After he resurrects our flesh, our bodies too will share in his risen glory.
40. Psalm 139:13-15, 17, 18, 24.

Part Two

1. John 10:10
2. John 10:3,11,28.
3. John 10:3,4.

Chapter Three

1. 1 Thessalonians 5:17—George Ricker Berry, *The Interlinear Literal Translation of the Greek New Testament*, (Grand Rapids, Zondervan Publishing House, 1958), p. 534.
2. 1 Thessalonians 5:16-19—Ibid.
3. Psalm 146:1,2.
4. Psalm 145:1-5.
5. Luke 18:1—Berry, op. cit., p. 213.
6. If I understand the Greek root of the word *hypo-piaze*, it indicates that the widow went at the judge like a hunter who harasses, ties, and knocks down his game for the take.
7. There are other New Testament texts that give a sense of "praying always"; these seem to me to follow in line with the two representative texts I have chosen here. Cf. Luke 21:36; Romans 12:12; Ephesians 6:18; Colossians 4:2; 1 Timothy 2:8 and 5:5; even Acts 26:7.

Chapter Four

1. Exodus 34:29-35.
2. Luke 2:25ff.
3. Luke 2:36-38.
4. Luke 2:19 and 51.
5. Luke 1:46-55.
6. John 4:34; 5:30; 6:38; 17:4.
7. Luke 5:16; other texts: 9:18; 9:29; 11:1; 22:39.
8. Luke 6:12.
9. Matthew 17:5; Mark 9:7; Luke 17:35.
10. Matthew 26:28; Mark 14:24; Luke 22:20.
11. John 13:23-25; 19:26.
12. *The Epistles of St. Clement of Rome and St. Ignatius of Antioch*, trans. James A. Kleist, S.J., Ancient Christian Writers, vol. 1, (Westminster: The Newman Press, 1949), "Ignatius to the Romans," section 4.
13. Ibid., sections 2,4,5,6,7.
14. Ibid., "Ignatius to the Ephesians," section 9.
15. Ibid., section 15.
16. "Ignatius to Polycarp," section 1.
17. *The Writings of Clement of Alexandria*, trans. Rev. William Wilson, vol. II, Ante-Nicene Christian Library, vol. 12, (Edinburgh: T. and T. Clark, 1869), pp. 432, 434, 436, 459 (Miscellanies VII, ch. 7 and 12).
18. Ibid., p. 434 (VII:7).

19. Ibid., p. 435 (VII:7).

20. Ibid., p. 438 (VII:7).

21. Ibid., p. 432 (VII:7).

22. Ibid., pp. 441, 442 (VII:7).

23. Ibid., pp. 462, 463 (VII:12).

24. *Origen, Prayer, Exhortation to Martyrdom*, trans. John J. O'Meara, Ancient Christian Writers, vol. 19, (Westminster: The Newman Press, 1954), pp. 46, 47 (Prayer, ch. 12 #2).

25. *Saint Cyprian Treatises*, trans. Roy J. Deferrari, The Fathers of the Church, vol. 36, (New York: Fathers of the Church, Inc., 1958), p. 158 (The Lord's Prayer, ch. 35).

26. Ibid., p. 159 (ch. 36).

27. *Saint Basil, Ascetical Works*, trans. Sister M. Monica Wagner, C.S.C., The Fathers of the Church, vol. 9, (New York: Fathers of the Church, Inc., 1950), p. 308, "The Long Rules," Response to Question 37.

28. Ibid.

29. Ibid., pp. 308, 309.

30. Psalm 76:4.

30a. I am indebted to Archimandrite Kallistos Ware for sending this citation to me. He has used it in his own article; "Pray Without Ceasing" in *Eastern Churches Review* II, 3 (1969). (from St. Basil's Homily on the Martyr Julitta, 3-4 in MPG, XXXI, 244A, 244D).

31. Particularly the *Life of St. Antony* by St. Athanasius; *Life of St. Pachomius; Sayings of the Fathers; Lausiac History* by Palladius; *Institutes and Conferences* by John Cassian; *History of the Monks of Egypt*. See extensive bibliography of "Sources and Related Studies" in Derwas J. Chitty, *The Desert A City*, (Oxford: Basil Blackwell, 1966), pp. 216-221.

31a. This phenonenon gave rise to the interesting title of an excellent book on the Desert Fathers by Derwas J. Chitty, *The Desert A City*, referred to in note 31 above.

32. *The Sayings of the Desert Fathers: An Alphabetical Collection*, trans. Benedicta Ward, S.L.G., Cistercian Studies, vol. 59, (London: A.R. Mowbray and Co., Ltd.; U.S.A.: Cistercian Publications, 1975), p. 18, saying 9. (see also Abba Isaac's experiences below: ch. 9, pp. 88, 90.)

33. Ibid., p. 102, saying 1.

34. Ibid., p. 198, saying 1.

35. Ibid., p. 34, saying 4.

36. Ibid., saying 1.

37. Ibid., p. 12, saying 30.

38. Ibid., p. 88, saying 7.

39. Two readings were the common practice in Egypt, but three—one after each Nocturn—was the monastic practice elsewhere. On Saturdays and Sundays through the year, and daily between Easter and Pentecost, both readings were from the New Testament.

John Cassian is the respected source for much of our information on the Egyptian monastic practices. See his Institutes, especially Book II and III.

40. Cassian mentions that the Egyptian monks did not celebrate Tierce, Sext and None as "separate hours and at intervals of time" but "continuously throughout the whole day, with the addition of work, ... For manual labor is incessantly practiced by them in their cells in such a way that meditation on the Psalms and the rest of the Scriptures is never entirely omitted." Institutes, Book III, Chapter II.

In Chapter 18 of his Rule, St. Benedict says that "our holy Fathers resolutely performed in one day what we tepid monks surely should perform in an entire week."

41. For example, note the following two apophthegms:

"Abba Peter said this about the holy Macarius: 'One day he came to the cell of an anchorite who happened to be ill, and he asked him if he would take something to eat, though his cell was stripped bare. When the other replied, 'some sherbet,' that courageous man did not hesitate, but went as far as Alexandria to fetch some for the sick man, The astonishing thing is that no one knew about it.'

"They said about Abba Macarius that when he visited the brethren he laid this rule upon himself, 'If there is wine, drink some for the brethren's sake, but for each cup of wine, spend a day without drinking water.' So the brothers would offer him some refreshment, and the old man would accept it joyfully to mortify himself; but when his disciple got to know about it he said to the brethren, 'In the name of God, do not offer him any more, or he will go and kill himself in his cell.' When they heard that, the brethren did not offer him wine any more." (Cistercian Studies, vol. 59, p. 109, sayings 8 and 10)

42. *The Principal Works of St. Jerome*, trans. W.H. Fremantle, Nicene and Post-Nicene Fathers, vol. VI, (Grand Rapids: Wm. B. Eerdmans Publishing Co., 1954), p. 248. (letter CXXV:11)

43. Ibid.

Chapter Five

1. Matthew 25:40.
2. Ghislain Lafont, O.S.B., "Note on the Spiritual Aspect of

Fraternal Relations," *Cistercian Studies*, vol. 9, no. 2-3 (1974) pp. 221-223.

Chapter Six

1. St. Teresa of Avila, *Interior Castle*, trans. by a monk of New Clairvaux, Fourth Mansions, chapter III.
2. Ibid.
3. I, at least, am capable of such distraction, judging from my past experiences.
4. St. Teresa of Avila, *The Way of Perfection*, Chapters 27 to 42. These chapters are sometimes published separately as a little treatise on the "Our Father," for example, *The Pater Noster of Saint Teresa: A Commentary on the Lord's Prayer*, trans. and adapted by William J. Doheny, C.S.C., (Milwaukee: The Bruce Publishing Company, 1942).
5. "Ladder of prayer" in terms of "lectio divina" goes back to a letter of Dom Guigo the Carthusian to Brother Gervase in which he describes the four "steps of the *monastic ladder* by which one rises from earth to heaven." An unpublished trans. from the Abbey of Gethesemani, Kentucky, (no date), bears the title of *The Monastic Ladder or Treatise on a Method of Prayer*, 8 pages. See below: chapter 10, pp. 117–120.

Chapter Seven

1. See St. John of the Cross, *Ascent of Mount Carmel*, Chapter 31.

Chapter Eight

1. Anonymous, *The Cloud of Unknowing and The Book of Privy Counseling*, ed. William Johnston, (Garden City: Doubleday and Company, Inc., Image Books Edition, 1973), chapter 7—this is the edition I have used throughout this treatment.
2. Ibid; in this quote, the words: "Use it to beat upon the cloud of darkness ..." must not be taken imprudently, lest tension and strain arise—which goes against the mind of the author. Rather, he intends that we simply refuse to *develop* any thought or idea, or to argue with oneself.
3. Ibid., chapter 3.
4. Ibid., chapter 26.
5. Ibid.

6. Ibid., chapter 4.
7. Ibid.
8. Ibid.
9. Ibid.
10. Ibid.
11. Ibid., chapter 5.
12. Ibid.
13. Ibid., chapter 7.
14. Ibid.
15. Ibid.; (see also chapter 75; and *The Book of Privy Counseling*, chapter 19).
16. Ibid., chapter 75.
17. *The Book of Privy Counseling*, chapter 16.
18. Ibid.
18a. from a personal letter of Dom Thomas (March, 1977).
19. Fr. William Meninger, O.C.S.O., six taped conferences on the nature and method of contemplative prayer:
 1. "Contemplative Prayer—What Is It?"
 2. "Contemplative Prayer—Who Is It For?"
 3. "Contemplative Prayer—How To Begin"
 4. "Contemplative Prayer—How To Do It"
 5. "Bodily Relaxation, Breathing, and Group Experience of Contemplative Prayer"
 6. "Contemplative Prayer—Practical Results" (Spencer: Massachusetts: St. Joseph's Abbey, 1975).
20. M. Basil Pennington, "Centering Prayer—Prayer of Quiet," *Review for Religious*, vol. 35, no. 5, (Sept. 1976), pp. 651-662. (The same references from *Daily We Touch Him*, Garden City, Doubleday & Co., Inc., 1977, have been added in parentheses.)
21. Ibid., p. 660; (53, 54).
22. Meninger, Conference 4.
23. Pennington, p. 660; (54).
24. Personal conference notes from Abbot Thomas Keating, talk on "Centering Prayer," (Conyers, Georgia: Holy Spirit Abbey, January, 1976).
25. Pennington, p. 661: (55).
26. Ibid., p. 659; (48).
27. Meninger, Conference 2.
28. Pennington, p. 661; (55).
29. Ibid.; (55).
30. Ibid., p. 662; (57).
31. Pennington, p. 662; (56).

Chapter Nine

1. Acts 4:12. Also Matthew 1:21–" '. . .you must name him Jesus, because he is the one who is to save his people from their sins.' "
2. The hymn is founded on St. Bernard's Sermons on the Canticle, nos. 15 and 47. For a comparison of the text of the hymn with the pertinent passages in St. Bernard see Ailbe J. Luddy, O. Cist., *Life and Teaching of St. Bernard*, (Dublin: M.H.Gill and Son, Ltd., 1927), p. 693. English translation of hymn here is by E. Caswall in the Roman Breviary.
3. Luke 17:13.
4. Mark 10:47,48.
5. Matthew 20:30; also 9:27. Note also the text Luke 18:13. In this case we have a parable of Jesus, not a live situation; and the Publican is addressing the Father, not Jesus. Nevertheless, the spirit of the Publican's prayer has been taken over into the Jesus Prayer, as well as the words "a sinner." "Be merciful" is the same in English, but in Greek it is not *eleison* but *ilastheti*.
6. Hebrews 13:15.
7. Cistercian Studies, vol 59, p. 111, saying 19.
8. John Cassian, Conference 10:10. Quotation from Nicene and Post Nicene Fathers, vol. 11, pp. 406, 407; Owen Chadwick, tr. *Western Asceticism*, Library of Christian Classics, vol. 12. (Philadelphia: Westminster Press, 1958), pp. 240-242. *Italics are my own.*
9. From an incomplete and unpublished translation made at New Clairvaux (chap. 59, 60).
10. Quoted by Patriarch Callistus and Ignatius Xanthopoulos, in *Writings From the Philokalia: On Prayer of the Heart*, (London: Faber and Faber Limited, 1951), p. 194. See also p. 222.
11. Timothy Ware (now Archimandrite Kallistos), in his Introduction to *The Art of Prayer*, compiled by Igumen Chariton and trans. by Kadloubovsky and Palmer (London: Faber and Faber, 1966) p. 31. Later, he says, in reference to the earlier writers, "There is no evidence that they knew the breathing exercises in their developed form" (p. 35, fn.2). This "developed form" is closely related to the hesychasm of the Athonite monks of the 13th and 14th centuries. The most that can be granted, then, at this early date is the possibility of an oral tradition and a handed-on practice that eventually came into written exposition via the monks on Mt. Athos: particularly Nicephorus, Gregory the Sinaite, Gregory Palamas, Callistus and Ignatius, and others.

11a. I owe this information to Father Kallistos, who says *ton hamartōlón* is found in the Life of St. Gregory of Sinai by Patriarch Kallistos.

12. *The Way of a Pilgrim* and *The Pilgrim Continues His Way*, trans. by R.M. French (New York: Seabury Press, 1965).

13. Ibid., p. 14.

14. Bishop Ignatius Brianchaninov, *The Arena: An Offering to Contemporary Monasticism*, trans. from the Russian by Archimandrite Lazarus Moore, with an introduction by Archimandrite Kallistos, (Madras: Diocesan Press, 1970) p. 81.

15. Thomas Fidelis [Smith], O.C.S.O., "Transcendental Meditation and the Jesus Prayer," *Monastic Exchange*, 5 (Winter 1973), p. 77.

16. Sergius Bolshakoff, *Russian Mystics*, Introd. by Thomas Merton, Cistercian Studies 26, (Kalamazoo: Cistercian Publications, Inc. 1977) pp. 236,237.

17. Thomas Fidelis [Smith], O.C.S.O., "*A Way of Meditating the Jesus Prayer*," leaflet (Pecos, N.M.: Dove Publication, no date). The same article appeared earlier in *Monastic Exchange* 6 (Spring 1974) pp. 55-57. It would not be out of place to say here that the Jesus Prayer is not strictly a "mantra." Fr. Thomas is applying the word loosely. A mantra is considered a prayer formula all right, but in the sense of an incantation. The Jesus Prayer is in no sense an incantation, a magical verbal spell or charm.

17a. Fr. Kallistos advises me that in the East the chief purpose of a prayer cord is not to count invocations, but to assist concentration and to help with the regularity and continuity of the invocation.

18. During the first day that I was using the bearing, I hopped over a muddy puddle in sunny California and accidentally dropped it into the puddle. I fished it out and washed it off, only to find that it wouldn't rotate as freely as before. The thought that shot through my mind was, "I'll leave you like that, as a reminder of my own recalcitrance and otherwise wounded nature." (Months later I got annoyed with it and oiled it. "Forget the symbolism.")

19. *The Arena*, p. 82.

20. Bishop Ignatius Brianchaninov, *On the Prayer of Jesus*, trans. by Father Lazarus [Moore], (London: John M. Watkins, 1952) pp. 78,79.

21. Ibid., pp. 83,84.

22. *The Art of Prayer*, pp. 98,99.

22a. Archimandrite Kallistos Ware, *The Power of the Name: The Jesus Prayer in Orthodox Spirituality* (Fairacres, Oxford, SLG Press,

1974) p. 4. How I wish I had had access to this fine booklet when I was preparing this chapter on the Jesus Prayer, It is unfortunately not widely known or available in the States.

23. *The Art of Prayer*, p. 27.
24. Ibid.
25. *Russian Mystics*, p. 271.
26. St. John Climacus, *The Ladder of Divine Ascent*, trans. by Archimandrite Lazarus Moore, (London: Faber and Faber, 1959).
27. Ibid., p. 258.
28. Ibid., p. 246.
29. Ibid., p. 245.
30. *Evagrius Ponticus*, CS 4, p. 18 # 12 (*Praktikos*, # 12).
31. *Writings From the Philokalia*, p. 412.
32. *The Sayings of the Desert Fathers*, CS 59, p. xvi.
33. *Writings From the Philokalia*, p. 33.
34. Archimandrite Kallistos Ware, "Silence in Prayer: The Meaning of Hesychia," in *One Yet Two: Monastic Tradition East and West*, CS 29, (Kalamazoo: Cistercian Publications, 1976), pp. 30-32.
35. Quoted in Bolshakoff, CS 26, p. 173.
36. Ibid., pp. 178, 179.
37. Ibid., p. 206.
38. Ibid., p. 267.

Chapter Ten

1. St. Athanasius, *St. Athanasius, The Life of Saint Antony*, trans. by Robert T. Meyer, Ph. D., Ancient Christian Writers, vol. 10, (Westminister: The Newman Press, 1950), # 16.
2. Ibid., # 55; *The Sayings of the Desert Fathers*, CS 59, p. 2, no. 3.
3. Ibid., # 3.
4. Ibid., # 2.
5. Ibid., # 4.
6. Ibid., # 45.
7. Ibid., # 73.
8. Ibid., # 44. In later life Antony himself was the great guide for younger solitaries and disciples. He could caution them against the wiles of evil spirits regarding their reading and meditation. He

alerted them to demons who would cause them to hear singing and
Psalmody, and to hear passages from Holy Scripture; and they
shouldn't be surprised if a demon tormented them by causing them to
hear the repeated echoing of passages they were reading (#25). In the
former cases, the solitaries might be elated and deceived that angels
were around them; in the latter instances, it was clearly to irritate
them and to disrupt their reading and rumination, and to stop their
praying.

9. William of St. Thierry, et. al., *Vita Prima Bernardi*, trans. as
St. Bernard of Clairvaux, by Geoffrey Webb and Adrian Walker, (London: A.R.Mowbray & Co., 1960), p. 58.

10. Ibid., p. 42.

11. Ibid., pp. 42,43.

12. Workshop excerpt, from *To Learn to Read Our Cistercian Fathers Profitably, Not Simply to Impart Knowledge*, by Dr. John
Sommerfeldt, 1976, p. 17. (Variant trans. in *Aelred of Rievaulx: Spiritual
Friendship*, trans. Mary Eugenia Laker, SSND, Cistercian Fathers
Series, vol. 5, (Washington, D.C.: Consortium Press, 1974), p. 46.

13. *Guerric of Igny: Liturgical Sermons*, trans. by Monks of Mt. St.
Bernard Abbey, Cistercian Fathers Series, vol. 32, (Spencer: Cistercian Publications, 1971), p. 214.

14. (Sirach 24:27) ibid., p. 214.

15. *The Golden Epistle*, CF 12, p. 51, # 120.

16. Ibid., #121.

17. Ibid., p. 52, #122.

18. Ibid., #123.

19. Ibid., #124.

20. Ibid., p. 92, #249,250.

21. See final note in Chapter 6.

22. *Monastic Ladder*, Section I.

23. Ibid., Sec. II.

24. Ibid., Sec. X.

25. Ibid., Sec. XI.

26. Ibid., Sec. XII.

27. Ibid., Sec. XI.

28. Ibid., Sec. XII.

29. John 14:21.

30. *Monastic Ladder*, Sec. XII.

31. For example, as a child, if I had been deprived of love and
affection, or felt that I had, I may be highly susceptible to indications
of God's love, and my prayer may be joyously volatile and find an
outlet in a considerable volume of words (*oratio*). On the other hand,

for one reason or another, I may under the impress of God's goodness, simply be reduced to silence in a gaze of intense love and joy
(active or infused *contemplatio*).

32. See Note 17 in Chapter 9.

33. Elder Paisius Velichkovsky, "The Life and Ascetic Labors of
Our Father, Elder Paisius, Archimandrite of the Holy Moldavian
Monasteris of Niamets and Sekoul," in *The Orthodox Word*, vol. 11, no.
4, (July-August 1975) p. 168.

34. Jean LeClercq, O S B, *The Love of Learning and the Desire for
God*, trans. by Catharine Misrahi, (N.Y.: Fordham Univ. Press, 1961;
Mentor Omega Book, 1961) p. 78 (quotations are from the Mentor
Omega paperback).

34a. Phil. 2:13 (New American).

35. *The Love of Learning and the Desire of God*, p. 78.

36. Ibid., p. 79.

37. I have experienced this prayer myself for periods between
1½ to 2½ hours, not infrequently, going back as far as my second
year of novitiate at New Clairvaux.

38. *The Golden Epistle*, p. 52, #122.

39. This comparison was culled from (with my own additions) a
report by Brother Ignatius of Mt. St. Bernard, "Symposium on *Lectio
Divina* and Study" in *Monastic Exchange*, 6 (Winter 1974) pp. 89-102.

40. Ibid., p. 74.

41. On Psalm 148, 1-2: CCL 40, 2165-2166. Liturgy of the Hours:
Vol. II. (N.Y.: Catholic Book Pub. Co., 1976), pp. 864,865.

42. *Song of Songs*, 2:11.

43. *The Love of Learning and the Desire for God*, p. 79.

44. St. Bernard of Clairvaux, *On the Song of Songs*, vol. II, trans. by
Kilian Walsh, OCSO, Cistercian Fathers Series, vol. 7, (Kalamazoo:
Cistercian Publications, 1976), p. 127 (Sermon 31:4).

45. *St. Bernard: On the Song of Songs*, trans. by A Religious of
C.S.M.V., (London: Mowbray & Co., Ltd., 1952), p. 230 (Sermon 74).

46. *The Love of Learning and the Desire for God*, p. 228.

47. CF 7, pp. 129-131 (Sermon 31:7).

48. *St. Bernard: On the Song of Songs*, op. cit., pp. 230,231 (Sermon
74).

49. Ibid., pp. 228, 229.

50. Isaiah 55:1-3 (and Rev. 21:6 "I will give water from the well
of life free to anyone who is thirsty . . ." also 22:17 "Then let all who
are thirsty come; all who want it may have the water of life, and have
it free.")

51. See note 15 of Chapter I. Ninth Revelation, Chap. 22, p. 60.

Conclusion

1. Ed. by William Johnston, Image Books Edition, p. 92.
2. Ibid., p. 93. (Emphasis mine.)